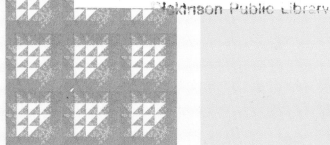

The
QUILTER'S
COLOR
SCHEME
Bible

The
QUILTER'S
COLOR
SCHEME
Bible

●●●●●●●●●●●●●●●

*More than 700 stunning color combinations
for every style of quilting block*

CELIA EDDY

kp **kp books**
An imprint of F+W Publications, Inc.
888-457-2873

kp books
An imprint of F+W Publications, Inc.
888-457-2873

A QUARTO BOOK

First published in North America in 2006 by
Krause Publications
700 East State Street
Iola, WI 54990-0001

Library of Congress Catalog Card Number
2006926435
ISBN-10: 0-89689-274-3
ISBN-13: 978-0-89689-274-3

QUAR.QUB

Conceived, designed, and produced by
Quarto Publishing plc
The Old Brewery
6 Blundell Street
London N7 9BH

Project editor Mary Groom
Art editor and designer Julie Francis
Copy editor Claire Waite Brown
Photoshop illustration Jurgen Ziewe
Photographers Paul Forrester, Martin Norris
Assistant art director Penny Cobb
Picture research Claudia Tate

Art director Moira Clinch
Publisher Paul Carslake

Color separation by Provision Pte
Ltd, Singapore
Printed by Midas Printing
International Limited, China

10 9 8 7 6 5 4 3 2 1

Contents ● ● ● ● ● ● ● ●

Introduction

How do you choose colors for quilts? It's a question every quilter asks. Teachers can explain basic principles and simple ways of selecting colors. They can suggest useful books on color theory, too, but, although valuable, these are usually aimed at people who will be using paint or other coloring media on paper. Working with fabrics is different and requires a different approach. The basic principles still apply, of course, but in addition you need a specific understanding of the ways in which the colors of fabrics are affected by pattern and texture.

That's where this book comes in. What you'll find here, first of all, is a brief introduction to the theory and language of color, with the basics of color theory explained in a down-to-earth and user-friendly way. Having that information under your belt will make it easier to decide why certain color combinations work and others

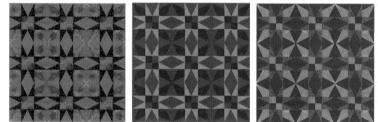

The Claws quilt, shown in seven different colorways, demonstrates the variation in pattern and mood achieved by varying the placement of colors and values.

don't, and allow you to mix and match colors to achieve the finished quilts you're aiming at. The heart of the book then lies in the 100 block patterns that form the Directory of Color Blocks. Each block is illustrated in a repeat pattern shown in seven different colorways. Classic American block patterns have been used as the foundations on which the color schemes are based, because they provide a simple but effective way of demonstrating the interaction between pattern and color.

Of course, this is not to suggest that repeat patterns are the only application for the color ideas and principles on which the book is based. All the ideas shown here can just as easily be applied to any style of quilt, whether it be pieced, appliqué, representational, narrative, or even an abstract art quilt.

Celia Eddy.

COLORFUL STEPS
Therese Bliss
A celebration of color in which each block contains colors that either blend or contrast, allowing only the value to hold the pattern together.

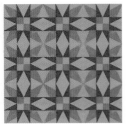

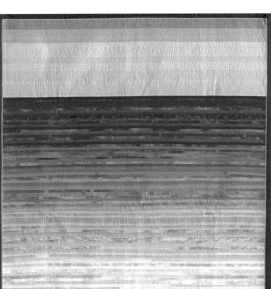

SEASCAPE
Dianne Firth
Colors and moods of sea and sky are captured in this quilt by building up strips of color, sometimes in subtle, harmonious gradations, sometimes using contrasting colors.

How to use this book

One hundred patterns, each shown in seven colorways, add up to an awesome total of 700 quilts. But don't worry, they're presented in a way that makes it easy for readers to find their way around.

The blocks are organized into five color themes: Harmonious, Complementary, Saturated, Tints, and Shades. The color themes have been selected to make it easier to choose and compare color combinations and palettes as you go through the process of choosing fabrics for your quilt. Each quilt pattern has a short introduction highlighting key teaching points illustrated in the various colorways, each of which is accompanied by a caption identifying the colors used and explaining what each one contributes to the scheme and how it enhances the overall look of the quilt.

Most of the patterns in this book use only three colors, although there are a few examples of two and four colors. Using a limited number of colors makes for

stress-free color selection and reduces the likelihood of mistakes. It is also a simple way to demonstrate the interaction of color and pattern, which, as we shall see later, is a vital consideration when planning a quilt.

Using the colorways

Each palette shown can be used simply as a recipe, so by finding fabrics to match the colors shown as closely as possible, you will know in advance how they will work together. If you're a beginner, this is the perfect way to get good results, because each of the block patterns shown will work beautifully as a quilt without further elaboration. However, each color scheme can just as easily be used as a foundation for a more complex and varied scheme, a "jumping-off" point, if you like, for developing your own color ideas or for creative experimentation with pattern and color. Use the guidelines and suggestions that you'll find under Color and Pattern, and Selecting Fabrics (see pages 20–29) to mix and match fabrics and patterns as you develop your own color ideas.

A brief overview of the designs shown on these two pages, comparing and contrasting the effects produced by the variations in values and colors.

Seven different colorways based on one of the given color themes are shown.

---

88 complementary/**Bear's Paw**

SEVEN PATCH BLOCKS

Whether you choose rich and dramatic colors, as in **Turquoise Points** and **Colors of the Indus**, or the cooler, fresher tones of **Plum Tree** and **Primrose Paths**, repeated Bear's Paw blocks make an interesting and complex quilt. In **Classic Red and Green** the complementary red and green make their usual impact, but the whole scheme is given a clean, fresh look by the addition of palest yellow.

complementary • **Bear's Paw** • **89**

1 **Field of Gold** The rich gold (1) provides a
2 background to the purple (2) of the grid, while
3 bright green adds a gem-like touch to the sumptuous, glowing quilt. The colors are of a similar tone so elements of the pattern have equal visual impact.

1 **Turquoise Points** Tomato red (2) set
2 against a background of rusty black (1) looks
3 rich and dark, while the subtly brighter value of aqua (3) adds a series of brilliant focal points and a little drama to the scheme.

1 **Plum Tree** Soft plum (1) and its opposite
2 on the color wheel, lime green (3), are set
3 beneath a neutral grid in a much lighter value of the green (2), which gives the frames around the shapes the greatest impact and casts quite a cool effect over the whole surface.

1 **Arabian Nights** Colors inspired by those
2 seen in Moorish tile decorations are of similar
3 tones, but the mustard (2) is just a little brighter than the soft midnight blue (1) and dark olive green (3), so imparting a lighter note to a quilt that might otherwise seem a little somber.

1 **Classic Red and Green** Traditionally
2 quilters exploited the vibrant combination of
3 red (3) and green (2) complementary colors by setting them in lighter backgrounds. In this case, a very pale yellow (1) is used for maximum impact.

1 **Primrose Paths** Blue (1) and tan (3),
2 highlighted by a grid of pale primrose (2),
3 make a color scheme that is fresh and crisp without any hint of prettiness. The lighter tone of the yellow ensures that the grid pattern dominates the design.

1 **Colors of the Indus** A sumptuous
2 combination of colors inspired by Indian
3 textiles, in which muted gold (2) contrasts strongly with deep purple (3) but less so with the rusty red (1), slightly subduing an otherwise exuberant color scheme.

Bear's Paw template This template shows the individual pieces of a block, irrespective of color.

Diagram showing how the pattern is drafted. Use this as a guide to drawing the pattern and making templates.

A brief explanation of how and why the colors have been chosen for each block, how they interact with each other, and the general mood and atmosphere they create.

Each color is identified in the numbered roundals.

Quilter's tip

Think of your fabrics as a palette, an array of colors to be used in a painting.

Color
for quilting

Ideas for a quilt can come from people or places, or simply from patterns, colors, and fabrics. Inspiration lies all around us. For example, natural landscapes, such as the sea, trees, gardens, plants, and woodland, are obvious color resources. As the English artist Winifred Nicholson observed, color schemes from nature are rarely discordant. She said "Flowers know how to accord their color to the color of their foliage. How do they know? . . . they are as mysterious to us as the rainbow itself."

The urban environment can also be a rich source of color ideas and patterns. Look at the subtle differences in the colors of bricks, slates, and stonework, for example. Simple things, like brilliant gold lichen on granite walls can yield unexpected visual delights.

Language of color

In talking about color, we use a specific vocabulary to describe its multifarious effects and gradations. The following definitions cover terms you'll come across in the descriptions of color schemes in this book.

Hue

The word hue is simply a synonym for color. If you have a collection of fabrics, a good exercise is to arrange them according to categories based on the primary and secondary colors (see The Color Wheel, pages 16–19), noting that red, for example, includes pale pinks, burgundies, and maroons, and that these can include light, medium, dark, bright, and grayed tones (see Value and Tone, pages 13–14). You'll probably be surprised to see how many fabrics you have in each category and how varied they are. The process may also reveal your predilection for one hue over some others, or that you are short of fabrics in one particular area.

Red and orange hues stand out against a dark background.

Various values and tones of a single hue make for contrast and harmony.

Fabrics come in all the hues of the rainbow and in an infinite variety of values and tones.

Value

Value describes the amount of lightness or darkness in the color and is a very important element in pattern-making. Each color has a gradation of values, ranging from the very palest—white—through to black. A hue that is close to white, for example very pale aqua, is described as being high in value, while when it moves closer to black, becoming a very deep turquoise, it is said to have low value. It is this difference between high and low values that provides the essential contrasts that make it possible to "read," or identify, patterns.

Hues that are diffused with white are described as tints, while hues to which black has been added are known as shades (see Tints and Shades, page 14). We use the terms light, medium, and dark in relation to any color as a useful shorthand to describe their relative values.

These fabrics, in a variety of hues, are arranged in gradations of value, from light through medium to dark.

Quilter's tip

Yellow stands out because it has the highest light reflectivity of all colors. Bright yellow with black is regarded as the most visible color combination you can use—think of school buses, and wasps!

Tone

Technically, gray mixed with a pure color produces a tone, but it is often difficult to define tones unless they are seen in relation to other colors; beige, for example, could be described as a tone of brown with a light value, while khaki is a very dark value of olive.

Tints

Tints are the result of white added to a hue, and they vary depending on how much white is used.

Blue fabrics in an assortment of shades and tints, ranging through dark to light values.

Intensity

Strong, pure colors are described as "intense," or "saturated," although the word is also sometimes used to describe deep tones of intermediate colors.

Shades

Shades are what you get when black is added to a hue, and they also vary in value depending on how much black is used.

Red fabrics showing varying depths of intensity and shades.

Monochrome

A monochrome color scheme is one based around a single color. The whole effect depends on using variations of value in tones, tints, and shades.

Contrast between shades of one color—in this case blue, ranging from very pale through medium and light to dark—is the essential ingredient in any monochromatic color scheme.

← Warm ────────→ ← ──────── Cool ────────→

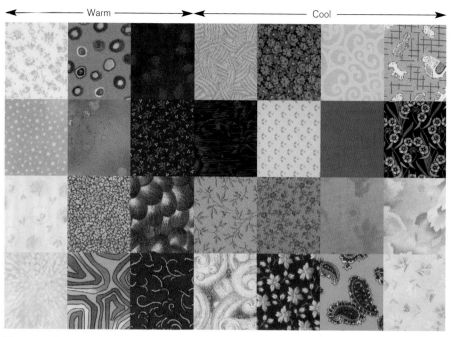

Temperature

Colors are often described in terms of temperature—warm and cool. Greens and blues, in their pure forms, are traditionally thought of as cool, whereas reds and oranges are warm colors. This is a useful concept in setting a mood or atmosphere in a quilt, or conveying emotion. However, temperature is one of the most relative and variable characteristics of color and may be perceived differently from person to person. Furthermore, color temperatures may be modified according to their setting—for example, deep blue in the context of a red with a bluish tinge may look quite warm.

Warm colors—reds, oranges, yellows—are separated from cool greens and blues by mauves, which can look cool or warm, depending on the colors next to them.

The contrast between cool colors, blue and green, and hot red gives this scheme a pleasing vibrancy.

The color wheel

A color wheel is simply a convenient way of showing how colors relate to one another, and is useful as a quick reference when deciding which colors go well together and why. A working knowledge of the ways in which colors relate to each other will inform your decisions and choices as you compare and contrast your fabrics, and the easiest way to see those relationships is through a basic understanding of the color wheel.

There are several ways of dividing the color wheel. The one we are going to use was developed by the famous Swiss colorist, Johannes Itten, who divided the circle into 12 parts. The circle is based on three sets of colors—primary, secondary, and tertiary—arranged in the sequence of colors in a rainbow.

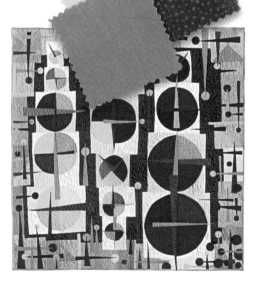

Primary colors

Red, yellow, and blue are the three primary colors, so-called because they are pure: they do not contain any other colors and so cannot be obtained by mixing. These colors, as mentioned in Language of Color (see pages 12–15), are often referred to in terms of temperature—reds and oranges are hot, while blues and greens are cool colors. This can be a useful concept when setting a particular tone or theme—for example, the colors and moods of summer or winter.

THE SUMMER DAYS, Reiko Naganuma
Bright primary colors—red, yellow, and blue—evoke memories of childhood summer days when the sun shone down glaringly.

ZINNIAS, Bridget O'Connor
Glowing orange and violet are set against green to capture the dazzling colors of flowers in the flower market in Seattle.

Secondary colors

The three secondary colors are orange, green, and violet. They are made by mixing equal proportions of two adjacent primary colors, so they appear on the wheel between those two primary colors. The two primaries, red and yellow, combine to form the secondary color, orange. Yellow and blue combine to form green, and blue and red combine to form violet.

Tertiary colors

The six tertiary colors are made by mixing equal proportions of two adjacent colors, one primary color and one of its secondary colors. For example, blue (primary) and green (secondary) combine to produce blue-green. In describing tertiary colors, the name of the primary color is placed first. Notice that in Itten's color wheel yellow, the brightest color, is placed at the top of the circle and, continuing clockwise, the 12 colors are placed in this order: yellow, yellow-orange, orange, red-orange, red, red-violet, violet, blue-violet, blue, blue-green, green, yellow-green.

INNER SPIRIT
Madeleine
Bajracharya
Rainbow colors radiate out from the glowing center to more subdued and subtle tones at the outer extremities.

Analogous colors

Any three adjacent colors on the color wheel are said to be analogous—for example, red-orange, orange, and yellow-orange. Used together, they give an impression of unity and harmony.

CLASSIFIED LETTERS
Ute Baunach
Analogous colors are used to unify and impose harmony on a complex block-based design incorporating many different, but related, patterns.

TRANSITION, Anne Tuck
Sky blues and complementary yellows, shading
through to glowing orange, evoke the transition
from bright daylight to golden sunset.

Complementary colors

Colors that sit opposite each other on the
color wheel are said to be complementary.
Complementary colors appear to intensify
each other when they are juxtaposed,
making blue next to orange more intensely
blue, and vice versa.

Quilter's tip

Try making a color wheel using fabrics from your
existing fabric stash. Notice where there are gaps, or
duplicates, and how many variations you have on the
three primary colors. Identify light, medium, and dark in
relation to other fabrics.

Color and pattern

The quilts in the Directory of Color Blocks illustrate the infinite ways in which color and pattern interact. Even simple, two-patch blocks, such as Winding Ways, can acquire great interest and complexity when there is a play on pattern and color—contrast in hue, value, intensity, or temperature can all have significant impact.

 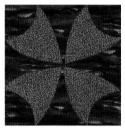 

Seven versions of Winding Ways showing the variety of effects achievable by manipulation of color, value, intensity, and temperature.

The lighter value of the petals brings them forward in a cool, gray-blue scheme.

Gold highlights in the dark background are picked up in the lighter, textured print.

Strong contrast between hues of yellow and turquoise makes a bold statement.

In order to see a pattern, elements of it must be defined and differentiated. In other words, they must be contrasted. Contrast can be achieved in a variety of ways.

Contrasting hues

Contrast in hues is a simple and obvious way to highlight elements of the pattern, and the quilts shown in the Directory illustrate the many ways in which contrast can be exploited. For example, when complementary colors of equal, or approximate, value and intensity are placed together, a striking impression of vibrancy is seen.

Placing red and green together (above) gives the stars clear, bright outlines and reinforces the generally upbeat mood of the quilt. Strong contrast between similar tones of complementary violet and yellow (left) makes the most of a strong graphic design, with touches of green adding to the lively effect.

Monochrome harmony in a soft fawn print with light coffee petal shapes.

Similar tones of brown and green create balance between the various shapes.

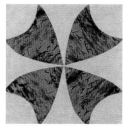

Pale sky blue imparts a light and airy atmosphere behind the darker violet petals.

Blue and yellow in bright, clear tones create a lively, optimistic mood.

Monochromatic contrast

Contrast is the vital element in successful monochrome quilts, which are created by judicious placement of varying shades, tints, and tones of a single color to emphasize the different elements of the pattern.

Although only three fabrics are used in these blocks, the graphic effect is strong because the contrast between them ranges from very pale through medium to very dark.

Quilter's tip

Keep in mind the words of the artist and teacher Maitland Graves, who said, "Contrast is essential to design. Variety stimulates interest and arouses excitement. A composition with too little contrast is monotonous, insipid."

Intense contrast

Using intense colors is another way to introduce contrast. The most extreme example of the way in which intense colors can influence a pattern is, of course, the use of black. Juxtaposed to bright colors it makes them appear even brighter. When used with medium colors, which are basically soft, black is still dominant but has a bracing effect on the other colors and helps to define them, resulting in a more sophisticated color scheme.

Black emphasizes the formal structure of the design, at the same time intensifying the blue and red (above), while intense tones of red and green get even greater impact from the addition of black (below).

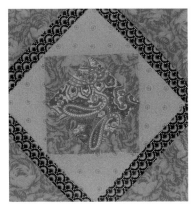

Contrasting temperatures

Contrasts in temperature can also be used to great effect and are especially useful for adding accent to a quilt. A warm, vibrant quilt, for example, may benefit from a cool, soothing touch. Equally, a basically cool quilt could be given visual stimulation by the addition of a small proportion of a warm color.

Brilliant green patches lend a distinct frisson to a quilt based on deeper, warm pinks and purplish blues (above left), while pink squares add a touch of warmth to the cooler blue (left).

Contrasting prints

Contrast in patterns on printed fabrics gives visual texture and can also add interest and complexity to even the simplest design. Strong geometric patterns in intense colors are a good choice for achieving overall effects of opulence and depth, while combining pretty floral patterns is a way to produce lighter, gentler effects. Fabrics with strong directional patterns—for example, stripes—also offer an easy way to introduce variety if specific elements of the pattern are selected and cut out.

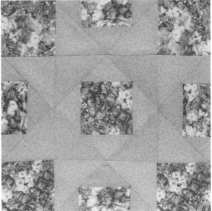

In the first block (above right), intense colors on a strongly-patterned print enhance the overall effect of an already complex design. A flowery print (right) gives visual texture to a light and gentle color scheme in the second, while triangles cut from a striped print fabric are joined to form the center square in the third block (below), giving much more impact to a very simple pattern.

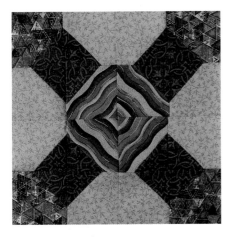

Quilter's tip

A good exercise is to arrange your printed fabrics according to pattern—large, medium, and small. Study the way colors are used in them and how they relate to one another. Identify those that would make good focus fabrics, and those that would be ideal as neutrals or backgrounds.

Selecting fabrics

Color theory is fascinating, but when it comes to quilt-making it is fabric, with all its variations of pattern and color, that becomes the all-important factor. Everything depends on the number of fabrics, the patterns, the colors, and the proportions in which they will be used. Function also enters into the equation, of course—if your quilt is intended as a bed covering or wall decoration for a particular situation, your decisions about patterns, colors, and fabric types may be based on the style of its intended home. Working like this, from an existing foundation, is much easier than inventing a whole color scheme, which is where you need to think carefully about your original vision and motivation for making the quilt.

Using color palettes in the Directory

Matching fabrics to specific colors can be tricky. If you have an extensive fabric stash at home it's easy to compare fabrics with the color roundels in the book. Equally, if you are going to dye or paint your own fabric, the roundels act as practical color references. If you need to buy fabrics for a specific project, "paint chips"—the color cards used for making paint selections that you can pick up in any home improvement store—are an invaluable tool. Thread them together so that they can be fanned out to display all the variations on any particular color. Place the paint chips against the color roundels to get a good match, then take them to the fabric store. Don't forget, also, the option of dyeing and painting your own fabrics, a fun activity that is becoming ever more popular—again, use the paint chips to decide on the colors you want to achieve and to check the final result.

Look for paint chips that match the colors you want to use as closely as possible, then use these to identify fabrics which match them.

Using patterned fabrics

With the infinite variety of specialist patchwork cottons now available, it's useful to bear in mind some basic principles about the way in which patterns work. The following is a quick guide.

Solid colors

Solid colors can be difficult to use in combination with prints because they tend to make either the solids or the prints stand out too much. On the other hand, used together in large areas they can produce rich, dynamic quilts, as exemplified by those traditionally made by the Amish. Instead of solid colors, try using mottled and marbled fabrics that are easily available today and are perfect for marrying with prints without calling too much attention to themselves.

Used together, solid colors can make a strong statement, as exemplified in Amish and Welsh quilts. Care is needed when mixing solids with patterned fabrics.

In both of these blocks, mottled fabrics enhance the light, pretty atmosphere of the quilts.

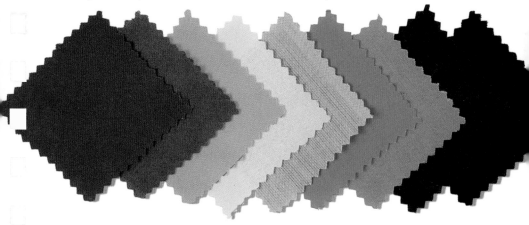

Large-scale prints

Some block patterns make a good setting
for large-scale prints—for example, in a
large central square that provides a focus
and sets the style for the rest of the design.
A large-scale print can be used effectively
for "fussy cutting" of motifs, or as a great
focus fabric—look at its background color
and the range of shades and tints in the
pattern, then try out colors that echo or
complement those colors, always keeping
in mind the overall effect or mood you're
aiming at.

Small-scale prints

Use small-scale prints as "support" fabrics
with larger prints or more assertive
multicolored prints to enhance or emphasize
a particular color theme.

Multicolored prints

Multicolored prints can often be bought in
sets as "theme" fabrics, also known as
companion fabrics, which can be very useful
because you know that they will go well
together. On the other hand, this method of
selecting fabrics does tend to take the fun
and excitement out of planning your quilt,
and can result in a rather dull and
predictable color scheme. You could try
starting with theme fabrics, then
supplementing them with fabric choices of
your own. A fabric in a slightly different
color or tone might add some sparkle and
originality to the scheme.

Large-scale prints, including animal
themes and a paisley print.

Medium-large prints, including florals,
abstract designs, and stripes.

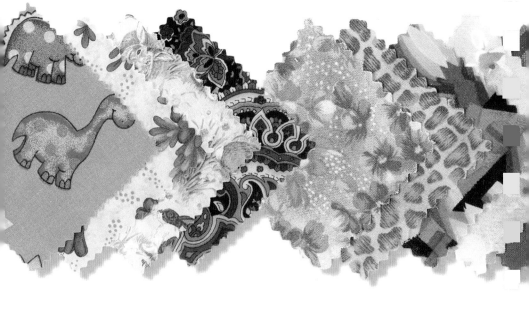

Other fabrics

So far we've been dealing with patchwork cottons, but there are many other fabrics that can be used, and each has its own special qualities that you can exploit to enhance both the design and color of your quilt. Here are some examples.

Velvet

A favorite of the Victorians and frequently seen in crazy quilts, velvet can be made from cotton or silk and is uniquely soft, dense, and rich. Although its surface absorbs light, the thick pile means that different effects are seen when the direction of the nap is changed. You can use velvet to add a touch of opulence, whether in quilts or garments.

BALUCH, Barbara Howell
Hand-bleached velvet in dark red, navy, and gold is perfectly suited to this design, based on a rug from Baluch in the Middle East.

Medium-small prints with floral and geometric patterns.

Velvet fabrics in dark and light values.

Silk

Silk fabrics can be found in a wide range of weaves, weights, and textures, which means that the finishes can be matte or shiny, smooth or coarse. Silk can be obtained in many beautiful colors and patterns, and can be used to add an extra glow to a color scheme. It's also widely used for dyeing and painting because it absorbs color so well. When using a fine silk, it's best to back it with iron-on interfacing before cutting out the patches.

Satin

With its smooth surface, satin reflects light brilliantly, so it is excellent when you want to add a luxurious touch to a quilt. It's worth noting, however, that satin is usually very dense and quite thick, so is unsuitable for hand quilting.

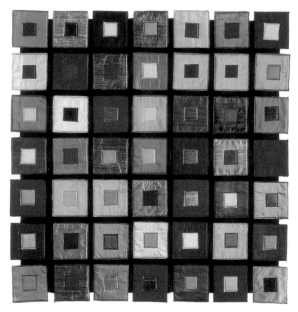

ON THE GRID, Joanell Connolly
The glowing colors and sheen of silk enhance an exuberant quilt based on a simple grid structure.

Plain and patterned silks have a subtle brilliance but need to be lined with interfacing to make them easy to handle.

Woolens

Woolens are available in a variety of weights, from fine wool crepe to the heavy weights used for suits, coats, and blankets. You can use wool in patchwork for items that you want to be hard-wearing and warm, but remember that washing may be a problem, so dry cleaning might be a better solution.

Synthetics

There are many wonderful synthetic fabrics available nowadays that are worth exploring. Polyester, nylon, and viscose can all be used, provided you bear in mind their strengths and limitations. Most synthetics are hard-wearing and washable, but tend to be slippery and more difficult to handle than cottons. You can often overcome this tendency when using them for patchwork by stabilizing them with interfacing before cutting them out.

This sturdy purple and cream woolen patchwork quilt would lend a sober, traditional feel to any scheme.

Satin has a unique shimmer that can add sparkle to any quilt, but it can be difficult to hand-quilt.

Woolen fabrics are always warm and practical.

For a really exotic look, brocades and fabrics with gold and silver threads are invaluable.

Exploring color ideas

There are several ways to explore color ideas for specific projects, so you can choose the one that suits you best.

Draft

Draft out your design on graph paper, then use colored pencils and pens to try out different color combinations. To see how repeated units will look, photocopy them the required number of times and glue the copies together.

If you have a computer with a dedicated quilt program, designing and coloring patterns is easy, and you can print out those that you want to use and keep them for reference.

Lincoln's Platform design drafted on graph paper.

Try out different colorways on copies of the outline draft. You can use photocopies for this if you wish.

Rehearsal

Another stage in the decision-making process is to "rehearse" various combinations of fabrics and patterns. To do this you need to be able to arrange and rearrange them, and view them from a distance, in order to gauge the effect of pattern, color, and contrast. Small pieces of fabric can be attached to a cork board, or to a piece of card using repositionable spray adhesive, to make a miniature version of your intended design. View your design and colors from a distance, preferably by looking through a multilens viewer or the wrong end of binoculars, to clearly reveal the effectiveness of contrasts, values, and tones. Move and replace fabrics until you are satisfied with the result.

Mix and match

If your quilt is to be based on a particular color, begin by choosing a focus fabric that contains a lot of that color. Look at the contrasts, brightness, and intensity of the fabric, and, importantly, look

Quilter's tip

If you have the space, cover a piece of soft board with white felt and fix it to a wall. Press or pin your fabrics to the felt and look at them from a distance. You can also make or improvise a design wall by pinning up a piece of white felt or sheeting–if necessary, simply draped over a door.

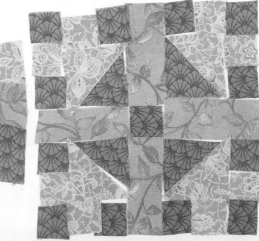

Snippets of fabric laid out on card using a light adhesive, which allows them to be moved around.

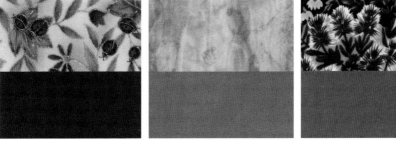

When combining plain and patterned fabrics, try to match the color of the plain fabric to a dominant color in the pattern.

out for any background color. If it is a strongly patterned fabric, look at the color values within it. What is the main color theme of the fabric?

Now choose other fabrics that combine well with the focus fabric, making sure that they provide sufficient contrast to define the pattern. Consider including an accent fabric to add a little sparkle, or a muted version of a color in the focus fabric to tone down a combination that is too vivid.

Although the quilts in the Directory are all based on two, three, or four fabrics repeated in the same place in each unit of the design, you can get good results by using fabrics that are not identical but are very close to each other in color and tone. Scrap quilts are often made in this way.

If you are not happy with the effect of a fabric you want to use, try changing the context in which it is placed—for example, a medium blue will appear dark when set beside a very pale blue.

Color and mood

In the West, moods are associated symbolically with certain colors, and you can use this idea to set the tone for a quilt. Cool blue, with its famous associations with melancholy and music, is also seen as representative of peace and tranquility. Red, the color of blood, is associated with danger and aggression, but also with cheerfulness and well-being. Green,

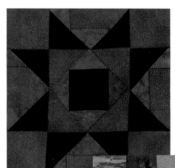

When red is dominant, it sets an upbeat and assertive tone. The use of blue is perfectly suited to a cool, watery theme, while green can reflect and enhance a garden theme.

Quilter's tip

Neutrals are fabrics in pale colors that can be used as backgrounds, or to separate more assertive colors. When in doubt about a color combination, try introducing a neutral. It may add just the right note of restraint, or serve to highlight a particular element of the pattern.

traditionally associated with jealousy, is also the color of growth and renewal. If you're aiming at a cool, elegant effect, then blues and greens might feature largely in your color palette, whereas a more upbeat, cheerful mood could be expressed through colors in the range of red, orange, and yellow.

Playing with colors and fabrics

Why not take the stress out of selecting colors and fabrics and have some fun by making up samples? These can be quite small—you can even use the little squares you get in fabric swatches. By playing around with colors and fabrics with no specific project in mind, you can learn a great deal about color and pattern combinations, rejecting those that don't work and keeping for reference any that please you.

Mixing and matching fabrics, and arranging and re-arranging colors, patterns, and textures can be a relaxing interlude in a busy day!

Quilter's tip

Another instructive activity is to look at the color combinations in paintings by artists whom you admire, and try to reproduce them in fabric, making up small samples.

Go with the flow

In the end, time spent with your fabric stash in a relaxed and playful way will pay dividends as you gain the skills and experience that will give you confidence when it comes to making the big decisions for a real quilt. And always remember, everyone has their own color perceptions and preferences, and that rules are made to be broken. Your notion of a beautiful color scheme may not appeal to everyone. The ideas and examples given here are offered as support and inspiration, but what you come up with in the end reflects your personal, unique color vision.

Directory
of color blocks

The Directory of Color Blocks contains 700 colorways, so whether you're looking for a particular color scheme and effect, or just browsing for inspiration, there's plenty to choose from. Use the different color themes as a guide and starting point. Looking for something light and pretty for a child's bedroom? Try searching through the Tints sections. For a more heavy-duty quilt, perhaps for a young man going away to college, Shades might offer better possibilities. Saturated colors are also excellent for creating bold, practical quilts, while Complementary colors are a good choice if you want to create lively, vibrant effects. Color schemes from the Harmonious section are always a good basis when a perception of unity and coordination is the prime objective. Of course, the patterns themselves can also inspire a quilt, so if you want to make a quilt using curves or appliqué blocks, you can find blocks of that style in the Directory. As you plan and design your quilts, use the Directory as a reference tool and as a rich resource, which will give you practical support as well as endless pleasure and inspiration for years to come.

Harmonious
Colors

Quilts based
predominantly on
harmonious colors have a
pleasing sense of balance and unity.
There are many ways to achieve harmony.
Monochromatic harmony is based on various
tints, shades, and tones of a single hue, and
is an easy harmony to create.
Analogous harmony uses colors that are adjacent to each other
on the color wheel, usually creating quiet, restful quilts, but with
more color and variation than used in monochromatic quilts.
Using complementary colors as the basis for
harmonious quilts can also be rich and exciting
but need to be softened by using tints or
shades of one or both of the
complementary colors.

harmonious/**Cross and Square**

Looking at Cross and Square patterns, sometimes either squares or stars seem to be the most prominent features, while at other times a diagonal pattern can be discerned. In **Country Garden**, placing fabrics 1 and 3, which are similar in tone, next to each other around the center square causes them to merge and form a border. In **Pale Stars Rising**, the pale cream fabric used for the points of the stars provides the main contrast so the stars seem to be the most obvious part of the pattern.

1 **Country Garden** Soft lavender (3) and pale
2 green (2) are echoed in the slightly darker
3 green-and-mauve print (1). The delicate
touch of lavender in the print provides
gentle contrast without disturbing the
general harmony of the scheme, evoking
the atmosphere of a summer garden.

**Cross and Square
template** This template
shows the individual
pieces of a block,
irrespective of color.

1 **Citrus Fruits** Fresh, light lime green (2), and
2 a slightly paler version of it (1), are contrasted
3 with a darker green (3) to create a cool
harmony. The position of the darker green
places visual emphasis on the squares rather
than on the paler stars, which emerge from
the background.

1 **Pale Stars Rising** Soft pink (1) and pale
2 lavender (3) form a harmonious background
3 from which the pale creamy yellow (2) stars
emerge. This is a gentle, tranquil scheme, a
perfect choice to complement a room with a
relaxing ambience, perhaps a bedroom with,
for example, a cream décor.

❶ ❷ ❸ Gold Star Quilt Subdued chocolate in a slightly mottled print (1), gold with a brownish tinge (2), plus a touch of soft beige (3), combine to make a subtly opulent scheme. The beige tones down the contrast between the brown and gold, maintaining the harmony of the design while allowing the stars' impact.

❶ ❷ ❸ Rain At Dawn The very pale grayish mauve (1) forms a background to the washed blue (2) of the stars while the darker mauve (3) provides focus and contrast. A soft and delicate scheme evoking an early summer garden in the rain.

❶ ❷ ❸ Primrose Path Harmony is achieved through the use of a dark leaf green (2) and a paler version of the same (3), set against a yellow (1) background. This is a fresh, cheerful scheme conjuring up visions of the flowers and leaves of spring primroses.

❶ ❷ ❸ Mountain Heather Pinkish mauve in medium (1), dark (2), and light (3) tones makes a tranquil scheme, with the darker fabric giving emphasis to the stars without making them stand out too much. The colors are inspired by the muted colors of the heather slopes of the Scottish Highlands.

harmonious/**Amish Style**

A simple pattern but nonetheless rich in design potential. In this example, the patterned fabric in the center square, repeated in the corner triangles, gives an interesting texture to the design. The long patches play a decisive role in the overall design; in **Olive Branch** they are pieced in a pale olive print that merges with the surrounding colors, whereas in **Orange Zest** and **Victorian Plush** they contrast strongly with the surrounding colors, emphasizing the diagonal checkerboard effect.

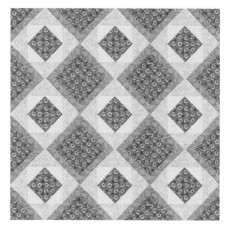

1
2
3
4
Olive Branch A subtle combination of two tones of brown, dark (3) and light (4), with olive green (2), echoing colors in the strongly patterned fabric (1) used in the center and in the corner triangles, which in turn adds textural interest to the overall design. A calm, restrained quilt with just a touch of opulence.

Amish Style template
This template shows the individual pieces of a block, irrespective of color.

1
2
3
4
Orange Zest The clear, bright orange (3) contributes a vibrant touch to the more subdued browns (1, 4), while the pale yellow (2) gives good contrast so that the effect of diagonally arranged squares becomes the prominent feature of the design.

1
2
3
4
Raspberry Ripple Medium raspberry pink (1) is separated from its paler version (4) by a muted mauvish gray print (2), which gives subtle but effective contrast between the two pinks. The clear, pale blue (3) picks up the faint patterning on fabric 2, to add a light, airy touch to a cheerful, summery quilt.

❶ ❷ ❸ ❹ Grove of Olives Harmony is achieved by echoing the dark olive green (3) and the paler yellow (2) that appear in the larger print (1). A soft, greenish beige (4) has the effect of toning down this otherwise bright and sunny scheme, reflecting the glowing colors of olive oil.

❶ ❷ ❸ ❹ Shades of Blue Tones of slate blue ranging from dark (1) through medium (3) to light (2, 4) are carefully arranged to enhance the pattern in this monochrome quilt. The dark blue squares (1) are made to stand out by the pale blue (2) that outlines them.

❶ ❷ ❸ ❹ Victorian Plush Rich tones of fuchsia pink (3, 4), with deep eggplant (1), could be rather somber, but the introduction of the pale, shell pink (2) lightens the whole design without detracting from its rather exotic effect. A warm, glowing quilt with a distinctly Victorian ambience.

❶ ❷ ❸ ❹ In the Frame Dark, leaf green (3) and nut brown (4) framing the center square tend to merge, becoming the dominant focus of the design. The center square-within-a-square, which is a distinctive feature in, for example, Shades of Blue, is much less obvious here. A strong design ideal for a utilitarian quilt.

harmonious/**Georgia**

Using just three fabrics makes it simple to create a harmonious palette. Choose colors adjacent to each other on the color wheel to guarantee a harmonious result. You can then achieve nuances of pattern definition in three ways—by varying the tones, intensity, or bias of the colors. In **Apricots and Cream**, the dark apricot fabric helps to exaggerate the checkerboard nature of the block. On the other hand, in **Emphasis and Contrast**, the brown fabric emphasizes the octagons.

①
②
③ **Apricots and Cream** Here, one color has been selected from the color wheel. Toning apricot shades (1, 2) are offset by the very pale cream fabric (3). This almost monochromatic palette cannot fail to be harmonious.

①
②
③ **Pretty in Pink** The intense fuchsia pink fabric (1), set against the very pale pinkish mauve (3), makes the crosses pop out over the quilt surface. The pinkish bias in the blue fabric (2) ensures that it blends with the stronger fuchsia pink to achieve a general harmony.

①
②
③ **Sweet Lavender** The lavender (3) and the pale pinkish gray (1) are both reflected in the stronger purplish blue (2), enhancing the overall effect of harmony. Using the dark color in the corners means that a pattern of dark octagons becomes the dominant feature, but with a strong pattern of alternating crosses.

Georgia template
This template shows the individual pieces of a block, irrespective of color.

①
②
③ **Green/Blue Hue** There is just enough green in the two aqua colors (1, 2) to link them so that they project forward from the bluish gray fabric (3). The darker of the two aqua colors (2) provides sufficient contrast without impinging too much on the generally harmonious effect of a cool, gentle scheme.

①
②
③ **Green Symphony** There is enough contrast in this almost monochrome green scheme to ensure that the pattern has sufficient definition. The pea green (1) and the light green (3) appear brighter beside the darker green fabric (2).

①
②
③ **Little Sparkle** The pale lime green fabric (1) adds a little sparkle to the color scheme without detracting from the harmonious effect, while the mid-turquoise (2) gives enough contrast to add definition to the pattern.

①
②
③ **Neopolitan Ice Cream** Two pretty colors, pink (3) and cream (1), are complemented by a pinkish chocolate brown (2). Variations in light and dark tones mean that crosses and octagons have equal value in the design but, as each of the colors has a pinkish tinge, the overall effect is one of warmth and harmony.

harmonious/**Grape Basket**

Effects obtained from this easily pieced pattern range from the fresh, light feel of **And Then Came Spring**, to the warm, rich ambience of **Soft Fuchsia**. Notice the effect on the pattern of changing the relative positions of dark and light fabrics; set into darker backgrounds, the grape baskets in **Floating Baskets** and **Lilac Mist** give the impression they are "floating" over the surface, whereas the baskets in **Warm and Earthy** and **Dusky Pink** seem to blend into the lighter backgrounds in which they are placed.

① **Sweet Harmony in Pink** The baskets are
② pieced in contrasting dark (2) and medium (3)
③ tones of fuchsia pink, both having a slight tinge of blue. They are set into a very pale, salmon pink (1) background to create an unashamedly sweet and feminine quilt.

① **Floating Baskets** Delicate eggshell
② blue (2) is matched with pale aqua (3),
③ which blend together harmoniously and are set into a background of a deeper tone of aqua (1). The baskets appear to be almost floating on the background of this refined and elegant scheme.

① **Warm and Earthy** Pale orange (2) contrasts
② strongly with the deep chestnut brown (3), but
③ contains sufficient brown to harmonize with it. The warm, earthy effect is enhanced by the soft terra-cotta (1) background.

Grape Basket template
This template shows the individual pieces of a block, irrespective of color.

❶
❷
❸
Lilac Mist The medium fabric (2) and the pale one (3) both hover between lilac and gray, blending together to give a slightly misty effect. The blue in the background fabric (1) tends toward purple, so that although it provides strong contrast, it does not disturb the general effect of harmony.

❶
❷
❸
And Then Came Spring Delicate spring green (1) and greenish yellow (2) contrast with the much darker olive green (3). The yellow adds a touch of sunshine to a cheerful, optimistic scheme, an effect that is enhanced by using the green (1) in the background.

❶
❷
❸
Dusky Pink Harmony is achieved by a gradation of tones of dusky pink, from palest cyclamen (2) through to deep chocolate (1). The darker colors (1, 3) steer the scheme away from the suggestion of sweetness that the pale pink (2) might otherwise convey.

❶
❷
❸
Soft Fuchsia The key to harmony in this warm and stylish quilt is the soft fuchsia pink (2) shading up to the pinkish purple background (1) and down to the pale, sugar pink (3). The colors blend beautifully, but with just enough variation of tone to give contrast.

SEVEN-PATCH BLOCKS

harmonious/**Bear's Paw**

Even in the harmonious examples of Bear's Paw the grid effects produced by the built-in sashings vary considerably. In both **Butterfly Bush** and **Tawny Glow** the colors used for the patches of the "paws" tend to blend together to form a background to the more defined colors used for the larger patches, causing the grid to appear more prominent. In **Blue Days at Sea**, the values of all three colors are relatively close, giving a more diffuse effect overall.

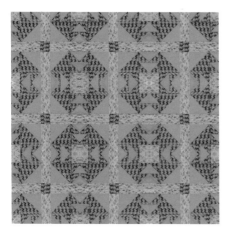

①
②
③
Blue Days at Sea Both the rippled blue (1) and the pretty aqua (3) are echoed in the darker blue-and-green print (2), and the colors blend to form a delightfully watery impression. Although the grid is unobtrusive it still imposes structure on the design.

Bear's Paw template
This template shows the individual pieces of a block, irrespective of color.

①
②
③
Highlights Rusty red (1) blends well with the donkey brown (3), which, in turn, contains just a hint of the grayish lilac in the very pale fabric (2). Although the lilac (2) is so pale as to act as a neutral, the shapes that are pieced in it contrast well with the other fabrics so are highlighted under the grid.

①
②
③
Butterfly Bush Two very pale lilac prints (2, 3) blend subtly together under the darker purple (1) of the rectangles, giving the grid the starring role in the design. Colors here are inspired by the blossoms on two varieties of buddleia—the familiar butterfly bush.

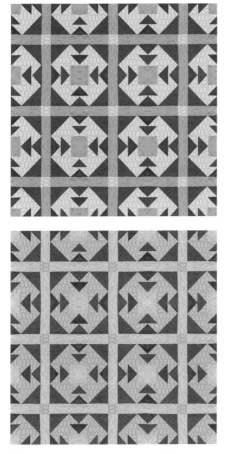

①
②
❸ **Ocean-going Quilt** Indigo blue (3) for the center patches makes them appear prominently as squares beneath the ultramarine (1) grid, while the very pale sea blue (2) shapes within the grid have definition without dominating the design.

①
②
❸ **Green for Go** Bright emerald green (2) makes the shapes below the grid stand out cheerfully against the more somber pale (1) and dark (3) olive greens, although the pale olive grid remains the dominant feature in what would be a practical, hard-wearing quilt.

①
②
❸ **Tawny Glow** Light hazel brown (2) and tawny gold (3) lie beneath a grid of palest coffee (1) for a quilt that has a gentle, autumnal glow to it. The grid effect is clear but not emphatic because the pale fabric blends gently with the other colors.

①
②
❸ **Beyond the Pale** Light (1) and dark (2) tones of eggshell blue are offset against a background of grayish mauve (3), with the pale grid allowing the underlying pattern to stand out strongly. This combination of colors is pretty without being too sweet.

harmonious/**Lincoln's Platform**

Subtle differences emerge in the secondary patterns formed by Lincoln's Platform when colors and tones are varied; in **Summer Berries** and **Warm Harmony**, for example, the repeated blocks reveal another familiar pieced block, Churn Dash, set between sashings. Sometimes, intriguingly, circles can be discerned where the triangle patches in the center and corners are pieced in muted, blending colors, as you can see in **Phantom Circles** and **Blue Sky Quilt**.

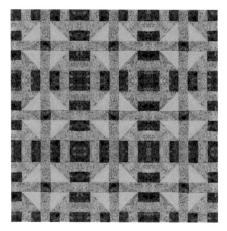

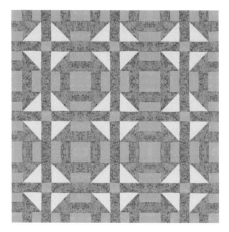

1 2 3 Phantom Circles Contrast between the dark green (1) and the grayish-green (2) print gives the illusion of curved shapes, set off by the pale green (3) of the large triangles. A hint of yellow in the print (2) adds a touch of sunlight to an otherwise subdued and tranquil scheme.

Lincoln's Platform template This template shows the individual pieces of a block, irrespective of color.

1 2 3 Plum Squares The dark plum (3) used in the center triangles, appearing as squares in the repeated blocks, gives them enough prominence compared with the background of blended lavender blue (1) and lilac (2) to provide a focal point.

1 2 3 Winter Hellebore With the greenish tinge of winter hellebores, the delicate cream (3) contrasts strongly with the darker leaf green (2) and the medium grass green (1) to create a lively pattern of squares against the blended greens of the background. A fresh, cheerful quilt to brighten a winter's day.

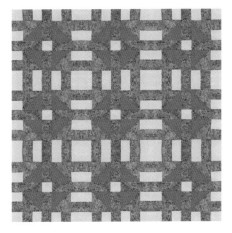

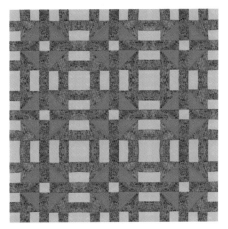

1 **Gentian Blue** Bright gentian blue (2)
2 contrasts strongly with very pale powder blue
3 (1), which provides the main graphic impact of
the design, emphasizing the horizontal lines.
The pattern of slate green (3) squares shows
unobtrusively beneath the grid.

1 **Summer Berries** Deep (1) and pale (2)
2 tones of raspberry pink form a background to
3 the dark loganberry (3), for a color scheme
with true harmony. Notice how the pale pink
(2) shapes join to form the main outlines of
the Churn Dash block.

1 **Warm Harmony** Warm tones of mid- (1) and
2 light (3) apricot harmonize with rich cinnamon
3 brown (2), which itself contains an echoing
tinge of orange. The brown corner squares
and triangles join to appear as Churn Dash
blocks.

1 **Blue Sky Quilt** Deep, slate blue (2) blends
2 with mid-sapphire (3) in the center of the
3 block, so that the squares are understated.
Horizontal lines set over a pale sky blue (1)
background appear to predominate.

harmonious/**Claws**

When the colors and tones used for the rays of the stars and the background are similar, the stars tend to recede, as in **Fading Stars**. In **Lemon Zest**, on the other hand, the strong, bright lemon rays stand out clearly from the surrounding colors. In **Veiled Stars** yet another effect is seen when, although the "stars" are well-defined, all the colors are soft and tend toward gray, imparting a generally diffuse effect over the quilt.

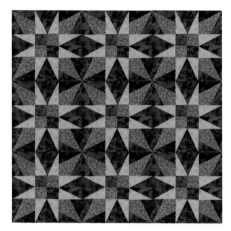

①②③ Fading Stars Colors from the pink to purple range on the color wheel are present in all the fabrics, so the stars' pink (3) rays merge into the pink in the mottled background fabric (1). The pale mauve print (2), although echoing some of the background fabric colors, can be seen clearly as a pattern of diagonal crosses.

①②③ Pink Stars Rising The lighter, rosy pink (3) of the stars seem to float above the pattern formed by the mottled, deep purple (1) shapes, while the medium gray (2) tends to retreat.

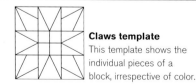

Claws template
This template shows the individual pieces of a block, irrespective of color.

①②③ Lemon Zest Two greens, one with an enlivening touch of kingfisher blue (2), the other a mottled, grassy green (1), form a background to the bright lemon yellow (3) stars. A harmonious quilt but with a lively twist.

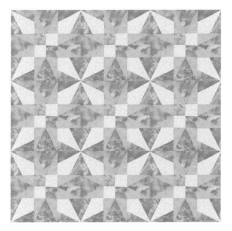

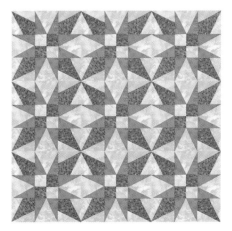

1
2
3 **Oranges and Lemons** Soft orange stars (3) seem almost to vanish into their pink (1) background, leaving the pale lemon (2) shapes to make the definitive statement. The diagonal pattern they create becomes the most prominent feature of the design.

1
2
3 **Pale Stars** Medium (2) and pale (3) tones of pink echo the reddish purple (1) of the background fabric, but the delicate pink of the stars is in significant contrast to the other tones, ensuring that they stand out brightly from the surface.

1
2
3 **Mocha** Pale coffee (3) blends beautifully with the mottled chocolate brown (1), while the olive green (2), although selected from another part of the color wheel, is gentle enough to enhance the general effect produced by natural, muted colors.

1
2
3 **Veiled Stars** All the colors are soft and tend to shade toward gray, imparting a gentle, misty quality over the entire surface. The medium grayish lilac (2) gives definition to the diagonal elements of the design.

NINE-PATCH BLOCKS

harmonious/**Puss in the Corner**

The dominant feature of this pattern is the illusion of a diamond-shaped frame, surrounding the center, with four squares lying over it. The stronger the contrast between the frame and the surrounding patches, the more it will stand out; this is particularly clear in **Echoing Green**, where the pale citrus of the frame, while echoing the greens of the other fabrics, lends a slightly luminous quality to the surface. In **Arctic Seas**, all the tones are close so the pattern seems less defined.

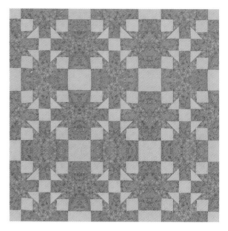

1 **Leaf Fall** Mellow, autumnal colors, in which
2 the golden brown (2) imparts a slight glow,
3 echoed faintly in the pale, creamy yellow (3).
Green with a hint of yellow (1), picks up on
the leaf theme for a tranquil color scheme.

1 **Streak of Pink** The streak of pink (3)
2 introduced to the warm, muted orange (2)
3 and its much paler version (1) enhances the
hot, sizzling effect, while the "frame" almost
disappears so that the two tones of orange
provide the main contrast and definition of
the pattern.

1 **Arctic Seas** Dark blue (1) and paler sky
2 blue (2) define the pattern, while the watery
3 aqua (3) adds a lighter touch and at the same
time hints at icy depths.

Puss in the Corner template This template shows the individual pieces of a block, irrespective of color.

 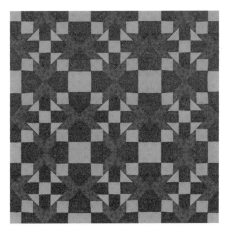

①②③ Lilac Time The pale pink (3) "frames" set the tone, emerging clearly from the medium (2) and dark (1) tones of lilac. A sweet, uncomplicated color scheme with a touch of warmth.

①②③ Broken Frames Pale pinkish gray (1) contrasts strongly with the purple blue (3), disrupting the visual illusion of a "frame." Set against the strong fuchsia pink (2), the scheme is rich and dramatic.

①②③ Pink Crosses Soft blue (1) next to the pink (2) causes a pattern of pink crosses to appear as the most prominent feature of the design, while the mauve (3) "frames" seem to float over the other shapes in this gentle but effective quilt.

①②③ Echoing Green Harmony in this almost monochrome quilt is not disturbed by the presence of the pale, yellowish green (3), which stands brightly against the other, dark and light, greens (2, 1), imparting a cheerful, sunny mood to a striking pattern.

harmonious/**Star of the East**

This classic star quilt is always effective and the harmonious versions of Star of the East demonstrate the wide variety of different effects achievable with even the simplest of patterns. The slightly faceted effect seen in the stars appears more pronounced when there is a strong contrast between the two fabrics used for them. For example, in **Midnight Stars** a clear three-dimensional effect is visible, whereas in **Luminous** and **Dusky Pink Stars** the stars appear to lie flat on the background.

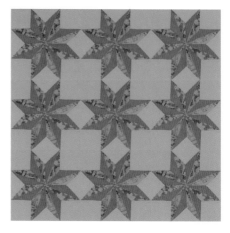

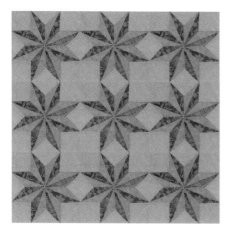

1 **Cherry Pink** The contrast between the
2 medium (2) and dark (3) tones of cherry pink
3 is muted and the dark fabric contains small touches of the background mauve (1); consequently the stars and the background tend to have equal value.

1 **Luminous** The rays are pieced in deep
2 turquoise blue (2) and lighter tones of the
3 same color (3), so that they tend to merge to form one shape. The brighter sea green (1) of the background imparts a slight luminosity to the surface.

Star of the East template This template shows the individual pieces of a block, irrespective of color.

1 **Pink Sky at Night** Palest shell pink (2)
2 contrasts strongly with the reddish purple (3)
3 of the other side of the rays, emphasizing the three-dimensional effect. The medium pink (1) of the background tones perfectly with the stars without detracting from their impact.

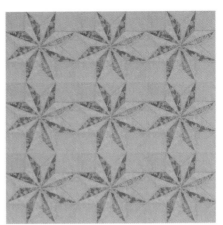

①
②
③ **Midnight Stars** Muted, inky purple (1) is the perfect foil to the strong indigo (2) and pale, sky blue (3) of the stars, which shine out from the background with dramatic effect.

①
②
③ **Dusky Pink Stars** Light (2) and medium (3) dusky pink tones emerge from a background of similarly muted lilac (1). Subdued contrast between the three colors ensures a soothing, muted scheme in which the darker pink adds just a touch of necessary definition.

①
②
③ **Autumn Glow** Tawny orange (2) and chestnut brown (3) glow against the pale coffee (1) background in a warm color scheme that would perfectly complement a room with a predominantly cream décor.

①
②
③ **Lovat Green** Soft lovat green (1) provides a gentle background to the stars, pieced in smoky blue (2) and a very pale sage green (3), which echoes the green in the background. The three-dimensional quality of the stars is just discernible.

EIGHT-POINTED STARS

harmonious/**Virginia Star**

By careful choice and positioning of colors it is easy to ring the changes on this eight-pointed star, in which each of the rays is pieced in diamonds. In some of the quilts, for example **Harvest Home** and **Pastel Pink**, strong contrast between the tips of the stars and the square patches tend to emphasize a grid pattern, whereas in **Lilac Haze** the points merge with the background color, so the pattern of individual stars stands out more clearly.

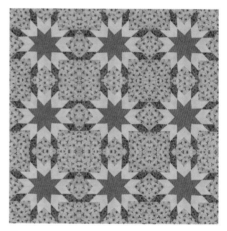

①
②
③
④
Harvest Home The mellow gold (4), dark leaf green (2), and soft green (3) in the star are all repeated in the background print (1), so ensuring a harmonious scheme. The dark points of the star join to emphasize the pale background squares between them.

①
②
③
④
Rainy Day Blues A hint of gray in the very pale pink (2), soft plum (3), and blue (4) imparts a slightly hazy quality to the stars, although they stand out well against the darker plum (1).

Virginia Star template
This template shows the individual pieces of a block, irrespective of color.

①
②
③
④
Splashes of Green The slightly brighter green (3) used in the center ring of diamonds gives them visual impact, standing out against the other, more muted greens (2, 4), while the soft gray print (1) fades into the background.

① **Pastel Pink** A harmonious blend of pinks
② (3, 4), shading out to pale shell pink (2),
③ are given definition by the soft plum (1)
④ background.

① **Russet Leaves** Warm chestnut brown (1)
② provides a background to the softer brown (2)
③ and glowing autumnal orange (3) which
④ surround and isolate the very pale peach (4)
in the center of the star.

① **Waters on a Starry Night** Pale blue (4)
② and two tones of sea green (2, 3) are
③ blended to form a translucent star floating
④ on a darker background (1), for a cool
and truly harmonious quilt. Contrast in the
centers of the squares lends them a
comparative brightness.

① **Lilac Haze** Pale lilac (2) points on the stars
② tend to vanish into the grayish pink (1)
③ background, leaving the two darker colors
④ (3, 4) to stand out like smaller stars in a
pretty, refined color scheme.

harmonious/**Bow Tie**

The strong, graphic impact of octagons dominates any design based on the Bow Tie block, but the corner triangle patches, joining to form a pattern of squares between the octagons, can also be a strong feature of the design. For example, in **Relaxed Mood** and **Golden Highlights** the squares are pieced in a significantly brighter tone, so that they can be read as a grid between the other shapes. In **Eggshell Squares**, the bright tone of the squares causes them to emerge as focal points across the surface.

1 2 3 4 Autumn Gold Earthy browns (2, 4) and beige (1) get a distinct lift when matched with harmonizing gold (3), creating a quilt with a warm, rich ambience. The dark brown (2) squares can be read as an underlying grid, lending unity and balance throughout the scheme.

Bow Tie template
This template shows the individual pieces of a block, irrespective of color.

1 2 3 4 Relaxed Mood Quiet tones of medium (1) and light (2) pinkish gray are a foil for dusky salmon pink (3) and deeper reddish brown (4) octagons in a gentle, relaxing color scheme, the reddish brown octagons acting as a series of focal points.

1 2 3 4 Eggshell Squares Squares of eggshell blue (2), being lighter and brighter than the other colors, become the main focus, popping out between octagons of jade green (3) and dark pine green (4), with pale grayish mauve (1) lending a softer note and confirming the basically harmonious overall effect.

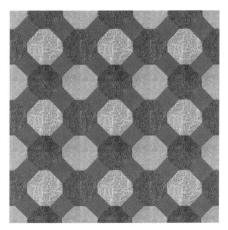

1 **2** **3** **4** **Woodland Berries** Woodland colors of nut brown (1), forest green (2), and golden olive (3) form a backdrop to the bright, rusty colored (4) octagons, which shine out like ripening berries on a bush, bringing a lively touch to an otherwise down-to-earth quilt.

1 **2** **3** **4** **Washday Blues** Emphasis is on the pale gray (2) squares, which can be perceived as a pathway between medium and dark blue (1, 4) octagons lying over charcoal gray (3) in a quilt with a restrained color scheme that would be ideal for situations where warmth and wearability are the main considerations.

1 **2** **3** **4** **Bright Fuchsia** A harmonious combination of two tones of pinkish purple (3, 4) with fuchsia pink (2) and dove gray (1), in which the slightly brighter tone of the fuchsia pink means that the squares can be read as a grid between the dark octagons. The gray contains a hint of pink, making this a warm scheme.

1 **2** **3** **4** **Golden Highlights** Palest green (2) squares act as a neutral, standing out against the alternating octagons of rich chestnut brown (1) and deep olive (3), and at the same time highlighting the octagons in greenish gold (4). This quilt would look perfect in a cream or beige decorative scheme.

harmonious/**Kaleidoscope**

One of the most fascinating and versatile patchwork blocks, Kaleidoscope can assume many different guises. When light and dark triangles are joined together, and medium triangles are joined to the lights, the pattern seen in **Warm and Cheerful** appears, with the emphasis on the large diamonds. In **Blue Circles**, dark corner triangles have been added to the medium center triangles so the blue shapes seem to join to form circles.

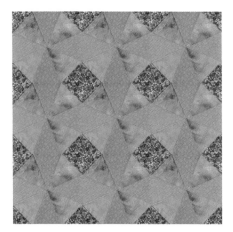

Harmonious Squares Harmony is achieved when colors and tones in the pretty floral print (1) in the corner patches are picked up in the other two fabrics—pale tones of blue and lilac (2) and medium pinkish lilac (3)—although the squares remain the focus of the design.

Kaleidoscope template
This template shows the individual pieces of a block, irrespective of color.

Warm and Cheerful Warm tomato red (1) squares are perfectly matched with pale pinkish beige (2) and nut brown (3). The strong contrast between the beige and brown give the large diamonds the main role in the design, which, overall, looks cheerfully crisp and clean.

Lilac Diffusion A monochrome scheme in which the dark (2) and medium (3) tones of lilac used alternately for the center triangles seem to blend, so the pattern is subtly diffused, with squares of pale lilac (1) serving to lighten and define it.

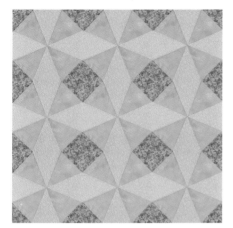

1 **2** **3** **Blue Circles** Three tones of blue—medium (1), medium/light (2), and pale (3)—are sufficiently differentiated to create the illusion of interlinked circles across the surface in a perfect example of a cool and graceful monochrome scheme.

1 **2** **3** **Fall Sunshine** Medium tan (2) and rich chestnut brown (3) blend harmoniously, creating an illusion of curves. The pattern is defined and the scheme lifted by the introduction of triangles of bright, sunny yellow (1), which join to form squares and provide focal points in the design.

1 **2** **3** **Spring Greens** Strong contrast between the spring green (2) and pale primrose yellow (3) results in a dominating pattern of yellow diamonds, although yellow and green pinwheels can also be seen. Harmony is achieved by adding the small print (1), containing echoes of the other colors.

1 **2** **3** **Morning Mist** A medium tone of hazy purplish pink (3) combines with a medium tone of smoky brown (2) to form subtle, slightly misty shapes that seem to link and interlink across the surface. The diffuse effect is emphasized by the addition of very pale gray (1) corner triangles.

harmonious/**Lattice and Square**

Various degrees of complexity emerge when harmonious Lattice and Square blocks are repeated. In **Gold Frames** the brightness of the yellow gives the long rectangles the major role, with the other shapes and colors receding into a shadowy background. However, in **French Lavender** a more complicated look is achieved when the green "frames" are muted, but contrast between the other two colors is strong. In **Fuchsia Bells**, the brightest color, pink, is used in the squares, so they become the focal point.

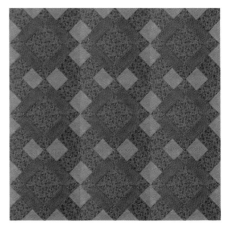

1 **2** **3** **Gold Frames** Tones of both green (2) and gold (3) are lifted from the medium print (1), ensuring balance and harmony. The long rectangles, pieced in a bright tone of gold (3), become the dominant feature of the design, emphasizing a pattern of on-point squares across the surface.

Lattice and Square template This template shows the individual pieces of a block, irrespective of color.

1 **2** **3** **Pale Constellation** In this cool and elegant scheme the dark petrol blue (3) rectangles, surrounded by a constellation of pale beige (2) squares against a very pale smoky blue (1) background, add definition and raise the quilt from the merely bland.

1 **2** **3** **Fuchsia Bells** Rich pinkish brown (1) and purple (3) tend to merge and retreat behind the pattern of fuchsia pink (2) squares scattered over the surface, which are just bright enough to act as focal points without disrupting the general effect of harmony in a very rich, warm color scheme.

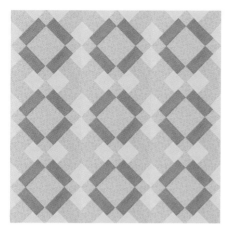

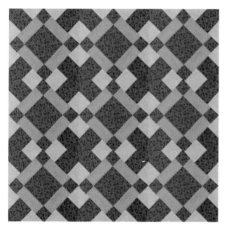

(1)(2)(3) Apricot Pie A warm, lighthearted scheme based on apricot (1) and a soft red (3) set off by clear, sunny yellow (2). Although the red frames make the main impact, look again and you'll see that a pattern of apricot crosses with yellow corners can be seen between them.

(1)(2)(3) French Lavender Dark lavender (1) forms a background for shapes in pretty pale lavender (2) and soft gray-green (3), so that different shapes and combinations can be seen: Sometimes a dark cross with lavender corners emerges, at other times green frames with dark corners are prominent.

(1)(2)(3) Meadowsweet A monochrome quilt in which contrast between bright, grassy green (1) and mossy green (3) gives the frame shapes definition, while the very pale green (2) acts as a neutral, lifting and brightening the whole effect while at the same time emphasizing patterns of crosses between the frames.

(1)(2)(3) Changing Weather Long rectangles in palest pearl gray (3) stand out among the surrounding blues; dark, thundery blue (2) for the squares and optimistic, bright sky blue (1) for the other shapes, which become a background to the pattern of on-point squares formed by the long rectangles.

harmonious/**Washington Pavement**

Triangles in the center of the block, looking like arrowheads or the "flying geese" pattern, can completely alter the overall effect. In **Arrowheads**, for example, they are so much brighter than the other colors that they appear to join and form a strong grid pattern across the surface, whereas in **Delicate Touch** they merge so subtly into the other colors that the main impression is of gray octagons and lilac squares.

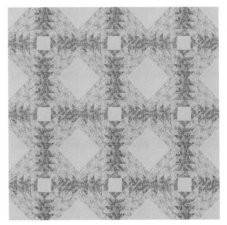

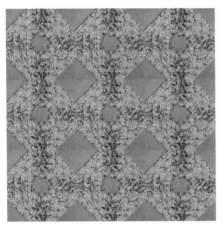

1 **Delicate Touch** Subtle contrast between
2 light (2) and medium (3) gray in the center of
3 the block means that the shapes tend to
merge, so that they appear as rows of large
octagons separated by pale lilac (1) squares
to give a gentle and diffuse effect.

1 **Coral Reef** Although the slightly darker tone
2 of coral (3) used in the centers of the blocks
3 blends well with pretty salmon pink (2), the
grid effect is still discernible, giving structure
and balance to the design. The warm,
understated overall impression is enhanced
by the background of creamy peach (1).

1 **Touch of Pink** Dove gray (1), with a hint of
2 pink, and pale sugar pink (3) are always a
3 harmonious combination, enhanced here by
the addition of medium violet (2) in a light and
pretty summertime quilt.

Washington Pavement template This template shows the individual pieces of a block, irrespective of color.

1
2
3 **Arrowheads** Triangles pieced in bright acid yellow (3) form a grid of arrowheads across a background of much darker olive (2) and rich brown (1), which are just sufficiently differentiated from each other to define the underlying pattern of octagons and squares.

1
2
3 **Rock Pool** Deep sea green (3) triangles look like strands of seaweed lying over pools of vibrant blue (2) octagons set with paler blue (1) squares to give a quilt in which cool blues acquire a surprisingly deep and rich ambience.

1
2
3 **Ripe Plums** A monochrome quilt based on three tones of plum: light (1), medium (3), and dark (2). The corner triangles, pieced in the lighter, brighter tone, come forward as large on-point squares, while small squares at the centers of the blocks look like little windows.

1
2
3 **Orange Pompoms** Neutral cream (1) squares appear between circles of orange (2) crossed by triangles in a deeper tone of orange (3), the contrast between the neutral background and the main shapes giving the impression of rows of circular shapes bouncing across the surface.

harmonious/**Winding Ways**

A remarkable number of effects are achievable with harmonious combinations, even in a simple two-color pattern like Winding Ways, from the cool, crisp **China Blue**, in which the lighter shapes dominate the design, to the more subtle and diffuse effect of **Twilight**, where contrast between the two colors is subdued. **Acid Test** shows that harmonious colors can be strong and eye-catching.

Woodland Ways Tones of autumnal brown and green are echoed in both the light fawn (1) and mid-brown (2) prints, the contrast between them giving strong definition to the pattern of repeated circles and petal shapes.

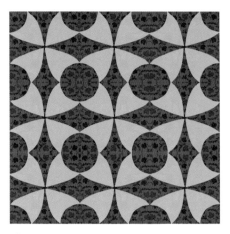

Twilight Hazy bluish gray (2) petal shapes are set on a background of dusky rose (1), but the brighter tone of the pink causes it to come forward a little more prominently.

Winding Ways template
This template shows the individual pieces of a block, irrespective of color.

China Blue A background of deep petrol blue (1) gives the maximum emphasis to the light china blue (2) shapes in a cool, crisp quilt.

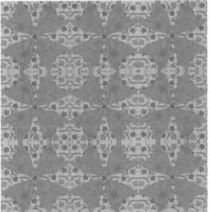

1 2 **Apricot Jam** In this warm and laid-back quilt, sandy yellow (1) makes a harmonious background to soft apricot (2), the contrast between the two being just enough to define the shapes without any of the elements of the pattern dominating.

1 2 **Peach Parfait** Pale peach (2) looks pretty on a background of light tan (1), which adds a soothing touch to a quilt that is the essence of warmth and harmony.

1 2 **Jade Garden** Smoky gray (1), which contains a subtle hint of green, provides a harmonious background for a softened tone of jade green (2) in a cool, relaxing scheme.

1 2 **Acid Test** A background of deep olive green (1) leaves the pattern formed by the bright acid green (2) petal shapes to make the maximum impact in a strong and eye-catching quilt.

harmonious/**Round Table**

Counterchange patterns like Round Table, in which the effect is created by swapping the positions of dark and light shapes in repeated blocks, provide endless opportunities to mix and match fabrics and colors, yet are an easy way to create striking quilt patterns. When contrast between the two main colors is subdued, as seen in **Floral Wreaths** and **Lilac Wheels**, the circle shapes are more subtle and less defined, whereas in **Eyebright** and **Four Corners** clear, strong contrast gives a much sharper, crisper look.

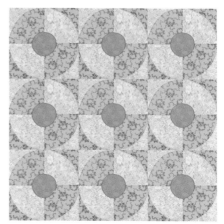

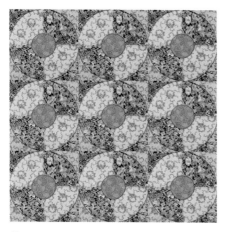

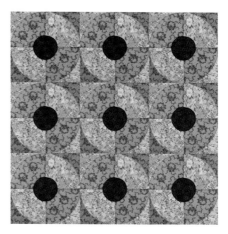

① **Floral Wreaths** A pretty salmon pink (2) has
② been "lifted" from the pinks in the floral print
③ (1), so that contrast between the two fabrics
is subdued, yet sufficient to give subtle
definition to the repeated circles, each one
completed with a toning gray (3) center circle.

① **Eyebright** A pale greenish yellow (1) tones
② well with lime green (2) in a clean, fresh
③ pattern of divided circles. A bright blue (3)
circle seems to rest on top of each shape,
providing focal points that enhance the
generally cheerful mood of the quilt.

Round Table template
This template shows the individual pieces of a block, irrespective of color.

① **Lilac Wheels** A quilt pieced in pale grayish
② lilac (1) and a deeper tone of the same color
③ (2) is light and summery, but gets a slightly
darker note from the center wheels in
deepest aubergine (3), which seem to peep
out from under the other shapes.

①
②
③ **Inner Circle** Wheels of reddish brown (1) and light raspberry pink (2) are topped by pale peach (3) circles, which make just enough of an impression to confirm and enhance the generally warm and comforting overall effect.

①
②
③ **Four Corners** Pale shell pink (1) and deepest crushed raspberry (2) look crisp and smart, an effect that is only slightly toned down by the addition of medium lilac (3) center circles.

①
②
③ **Amber Eyes** Pale, greenish yellow (1) and a deep olive green (2) tone well together, the brighter yellow giving a crisp, lively feel to the quilt, while the amber (3) circles provide a series of lively focal points across the surface.

①
②
③ **Skyscape** Subdued contrast between sky blue (1) and cloudy gray (2) means that the overall effect of the quartered circles is muted. However, deep midnight blue (3) circles, appearing from below the other shapes, provide focal points that sharpen and define the design.

FAN BLOCKS

harmonious/**Japanese Fan**

Four Japanese Fan blocks rotated and joined make a striking, wheel-like pattern that can be as versatile as you like. **Sapphire Glow** is rich and dark, while **Touch of Violet** is light and pretty. When the main part of the fan is pieced in well-contrasted tones, as in **Crocodile Skin** and **Checkered Fans**, the design has both visual texture and graphic impact. **Gray Skies Fans** has a subtle harmony, but is enhanced by the darker rings at the centers and the strips lying between the fans and the background.

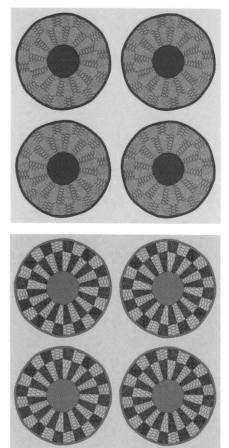

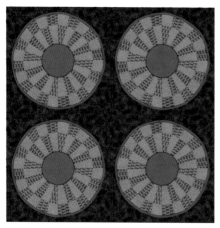

①②③④ Sapphire Glow Set on a background of deep sapphire blue (1), fans pieced in medium turquoise (2) and a lighter, textured blue (3) look rich and glowing. Outlining the wheels in medium blue (4) gives just enough definition to the main shapes without detracting from the harmonious overall effect.

Japanese Fan template
This template shows the individual pieces of a block, irrespective of color.

①②③④ Touch of Violet A touch of deep violet (4) for the smaller center circles and edges of the main circles gives emphasis to the main shapes and makes a clear division between the rotated fans, pieced in lilac (2) and medium lavender (3), and the shell pink (1) background, making a light, summery quilt.

①②③④ Crocodile Skin The fans in each block are pieced in dark olive (2) and a lighter, textured tone of the same color (3), giving them a slightly scaly, textured look. Center circles and outlining strips in fawn brown (4) give subtle definition to the main shapes when placed on a neutral background of palest olive (1).

①②③④ Fiery Fans Hot tomato red (2) and orange (3), set on a background of rich chestnut brown (1), could be a little hard on the eye, but pale coffee (4) circles and outline strips are just the right tone to add a calming touch to a warm and vibrant quilt.

①②③④ Checkered Fans Alternating dark blue (2) and pale grayish blue (3) in the fan patches make for a strong graphic statement, with dark gray (4) circles and outline strips acting simply as boundaries between the fan and the toning sky blue (1) background.

①②③④ Fallen Leaves There's a hint of fall in the two tones of orange (2, 3) set against a background of dark hazel brown (1). The misty gray (4) circles and strips give soft definition and emphasize the generally autumnal ambience.

①②③④ Gray Skies Fans Light sugar pink (2) and medium pink (3) combined in pretty, understated fan shapes make a much stronger impact when bounded by deep aubergine (4) strips and set against a rainy sky background of pearly gray (1) in a gentle, feminine quilt with a touch of elegance.

harmonious/**Friendship Fan**

Four Friendship Fan blocks are pieced and joined with the arcs in the center to make a striking pattern. Two harmonizing colors give unity and balance, but a carefully chosen third color can still impact on the final effect. In **Sunset Streaks**, the addition of a small proportion of pink adds to the warm and glowing effects, while in **Striped Green**, an example of a more assertive use of two harmonious colors, the third color, apricot, is deliberately chosen to enhance and exaggerate the clear-cut impression of the scheme.

1 **2** **3** **Spring Echoes** The sweet, spring-like colors in the pale floral print (1) are echoed in a deeper grassy green (2), while the pretty violet (3), also echoed in the floral print, adds a gently contrasting note without disturbing the overall effect of cheerful harmony.

1 **2** **3** **Two-tone Lavender** Two tones of lavender, deep (1) and medium (2), make a softly harmonious combination, set off and emphasized by contrast with splashes of fresh aqua (3) in the circles across the surface.

Friendship Fan template This template shows the individual pieces of a block, irrespective of color.

1 **2** **3** **Sunset Streaks** Medium peach (1) with soft orange (2) reflect the colors of a vivid sunset in a warm, sunny quilt, with a dash of pink (3) to add the necessary division between the main shapes and the circles, as well as adding yet another tone to the sunset theme.

①
②
③
Cool Harmony Cool lime (2) casts a refreshing atmosphere on the more subdued colors of soft green with a hint of gray (1) and brown (3), which contains a suggestion of green, so that harmony is maintained in a quilt with a cool and elegant feel to it.

①
②
③
Subtle Harmony Turquoise blue (1) and smoky grayish blue (2) are subtly harmonious, although the grayish blue, being in a lighter tone, tends to make the greatest impact. Deep purple (3) gives just enough definition to the center circles.

①
②
③
Dusky Rose Rosy pink (2) sets a light, bright tone, but matched with darker, duskier pink (1) the quilt looks more warm and rich than pretty, an impression that is confirmed and enhanced by the violet (3) rings.

①
②
③
Striped Green Well-defined contrast between the dark green (1) and apple green (2) make for a strong, clear-cut effect, although using the paler green as the main color ensures a generally light impression. Apricot (3) rings make for a series of lively focal points among the harmonizing greens.

APPLIQUÉ BLOCKS

harmonious/**Bleeding Hearts**

Bleeding Hearts is a curved pattern with infinite design potential; indeed, sometimes it's difficult to believe that all the quilts shown are the same pattern. In **Shadow Dance** and **Winter Sage** the circles are almost lost as the petal shapes are emphasized. In **Early Spring**, because the three colors are similar in tone, all the shapes emerge, while in **Pink Dishes** and **Echoing Green** the petal pattern shows up against a clear pattern of circles separated by diamond shapes.

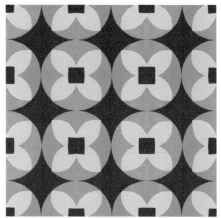

1 2 3 **Shadow Dance** A muted scheme in which harmony is achieved because the medium lavender gray (2) holds just a suggestion of the pink (3), with pale slatey gray (1) underscoring the slightly shadowy overall effect.

1 2 3 **Winter Sage** Shapes in icy blue (1) and pale sage green (3) are almost lost, forming a shadowy background to the petal shapes in deeper green (2), which become the main focus in a cool, elegant quilt.

Bleeding Hearts template This template shows the individual pieces of a block, irrespective of color.

1 2 3 **Pink Dishes** Pale pink (2) petals seem to lie on circles of deeper, cyclamen pink (3), which gain maximum emphasis when juxtaposed against deep, rich burgundy (1) in a quilt that has a strong graphic impact because all the shapes are clear and well-defined.

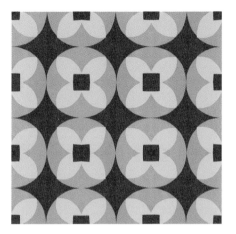

1 **Petal Power** Light acid yellow (2) petal
2 shapes are set against greenish gray (3)
3 circles that contrast well with deep olive (1)
in a well-balanced, harmonious quilt.

1 **Fruit Squash** Subdued contrast between
2 tangerine (1) and muted apricot (3) leaves
3 the brighter lemon yellow (2) petal shapes
to make the main impact in a delightfully
warm and sunny quilt.

1 **Early Spring** Light-hearted pastel tones of
2 lime (1) and spearmint green (3) are a perfect
3 foil for the very slightly brighter daffodil yellow
(2) petal shapes, which come forward to give
focus without detracting from the generally
harmonious effect.

1 **Echoing Green** Medium jade (1) finds an
2 echo in both vibrant kingfisher blue (2) and
3 deep petrol blue (3), but its brighter tone
emphasizes the small squares and larger
curve-sided shapes, which stand out between
the circles formed by the shapes in the other
two colors.

harmonious/**Dutch Tulips**

In repeated Dutch Tulips blocks, the flower heads form curve-sided squares, although other pattern elements may dominate the design. In **Blue Lanterns**, for example, it is the shapes made where the blue-gray backgrounds meet that predominate. With **Light and Airy**, the brighter tone of the pink tulip heads ensures that those shapes come forward, while in **Ginger Spice**, the contrast between the subdued brown background and the pale gray and peach of the leaves, stems, and centers means that those shapes are strongest.

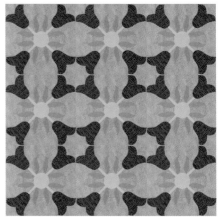

1 2 3 4 **Summer Gold** The golden honey (1) background merges with the medium gold (2) of the tulip heads, forming a swirling pattern behind leaf and stem shapes in dark tan (3) and burnt orange (4), so that the pattern they make stands out across the surface as a series of daisy heads.

1 2 3 4 **Lemon Zest** A contrast between the background olive (1) and lime green (2) gives a well-defined pattern of curved shapes across the surface of the quilt, with medium brown (4) serving as a foil to the pale yellow (3) leaves, which therefore become a series of bright focal points.

1 2 3 4 **Blue Lanterns** In this unusual interpretation of the Tulip design, a variety of patterns emerge when misty gray (1) backgrounds join to form a series of lantern-like shapes, alternating with curved, four-sided shapes in indigo blue (2) and florets of bluish green (3) and powder blue (4), in a cool, elegant quilt.

Dutch Tulips template
This template shows the individual pieces of a block, irrespective of color.

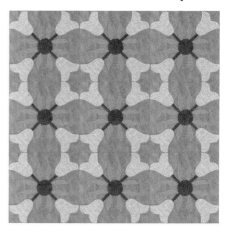

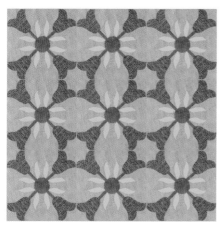

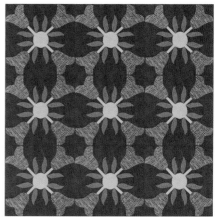

①②③④ Ginger Spice Softened tones of earthy brown (1) are a foil for the lighter, brighter gray (3) leaves and peach (4) stems and centers, with the ginger (2) used for the tulip heads adding a little spice to a warm, soothing color scheme.

①②③④ Spring Shower There is a soft, natural feel to this combination of soft gray-green (1) for the background, set with darker, olive green (2) tulip heads, light grass green (3) leaves and even darker green (4) stems and centers.

①②③④ Light and Airy Curve-sided squares of sweet pastel pink (2) flower heads alternate with florets of deeper pink (3) leaves and crushed raspberry (4) stems and centers, on a background of soft and airy bluish lilac (1) in a charmingly light, feminine color scheme.

①②③④ Deep Violet In a quilt with a subtly exotic feel to it, a sumptuous tone of deep violet (1) combines with a lighter, harmonizing tone of violet (2) to make shapes that recede a little behind leaves of dusky pink (3) and very much brighter stems and center circles in pale pink (4).

Complementary
Colors

Complementary colors
are those that lie on
opposite sides of the color wheel.
Red is complementary to green, blue to
orange, and violet to yellow. When
complementary colors of similar value and
intensity are juxtaposed, they seem to intensify each
other so that startling "vibrations" appear at their edges.
Complementaries also affect other colors so that, for example,
when a blue-green fabric is placed against a strong red fabric
it will appear more green than blue, but place it against
orange and its blueness will be heightened.
The effect of complementary colors can
be moderated by the addition of more
subdued tones.

complementary/**Cross and Square**

Cross and Square is a classic star block, but the stars, seen clearly in **Golden Stars**, are not always a strong feature of the design; in **Tangerine Dream** and **Emerald Squares**, for example, the squares catch the eye first, and in **Gold Highlights**, the dark patches tend to merge to form large crosses. The large squares that appear where the blocks meet provide an opportunity to enhance the quilt with a quilting design.

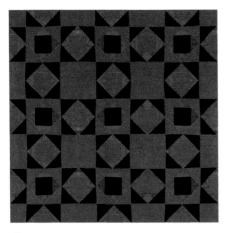

① **Gem Quilt** The brilliance of ruby red (1) and
② emerald green (3) is enhanced when black
③ (2) is introduced. A strong, vibrant quilt that might complement a Victorian-style room, or one for a teenager.

① **Golden Stars** Complementary blue (3) and
② golden yellow (2) both contrast well with the
③ dark tan (1), but the yellow stars make the greatest impact while the blue acts as a foil to both the other colors.

① **Warm and Cool** A very pale primrose yellow
② (3) acts as a neutral in a scheme based on
3 cool, mid-aqua (2) and its opposite on the color wheel, warm tan (1), emphasizing the diagonal direction of the pattern in a restrained and elegant color scheme.

Cross and Square template This template shows the individual pieces of a block, irrespective of color.

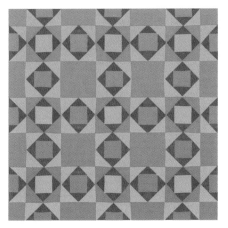

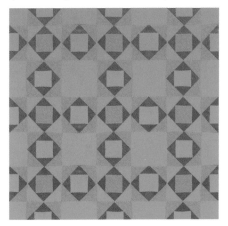

1 2 3 **Tangerine Dream** Bright orange (1) set in two shades of its complementary color blue (2, 3), makes for a strong and vibrant effect. The pattern of squares-within-squares predominates, so you really have to look for the stars.

1 2 3 **Emerald Squares** Brilliant cyclamen pink (3) and complementary emerald green (1) are matched with deep blue (2), which sits between them on the color wheel, resulting in a rich color scheme in which green squares appear to dominate. The smaller proportion of cyclamen contributes a warm, lively touch.

1 2 3 **Vibrant Effect** Grassy green (1) with an almost complementary deep violet (3) are matched with a bright, electric blue (2) to vibrant effect. The pattern of large green squares alternating with squares-within-squares dominates the design.

1 2 3 **Gold Highlights** The very dark plum (1) and lighter plum color (2) tend to merge to form a diagonal pattern of crosses, with the bright gold (3) providing a pattern of highlights across the surface in a rich, glowing color scheme.

complementary/**Amish Style**

Even pale and muted tones of complementary colors have resonance; in **Pink Frames** the pale pink contrasts strongly with the green, making the frames really stand out. In **Bright and Breezy**, all the colors are of similar tones, giving equal emphasis to each element of the pattern so that a strong checkerboard effect emerges. More subtle effects appear when the neutrals are introduced, as in **Cherry Pie**.

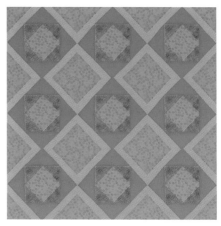

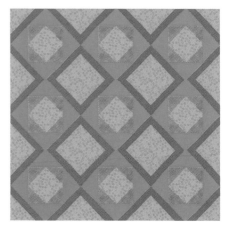

Bright and Breezy A dynamic color scheme unified by the orange print (1), which is patterned with all the other colors. Bright blue (4) contrasts with complementary yellow (3) and turquoise (2) with orange (1) in a bright and breezy quilt in seaside colors.

Amber Lights A splash of amber (4) adds a lively touch to the neutral gray (2) and to the cool colors, turquoise (1) and green (3), in an otherwise restrained color scheme. The turquoise squares stand out well against both the complementary amber background and the gray, giving them the major role.

Cherry Pie Cherry pink (2) juxtaposed to complementary mid-green (3) ensures that the diagonally set "windows" make maximum impact on the design, the softer tones of lovat green (1) and rose pink (4) casting a slightly subdued and calming ambience.

Amish Style template
This template shows the individual pieces of a block, irrespective of color.

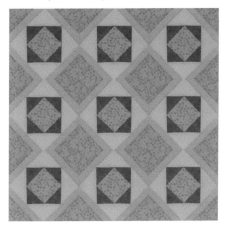

1 2 3 4 High Summer Combinations of complementary green (2) and brick red (3), yellow (1) and purple (4), create a vibrant, sunny quilt reflecting the colors of high summer. The main focus is on the yellow squares outlined both by green and purple.

1 2 3 4 Resonating Colors Focus is on the red (4) and aquamarine (1) in the center square, where the combination of warm and cool colors resonates. The final effect is softened by the surrounding neutral gray (2), with a light pink (3) adding a fresh, lively touch to the scheme.

1 2 3 4 Kingfisher Windows Glowing orange (2), framing the larger squares, contrasts well with both the Kingfisher blue (1) and purple (4). The softer olive (3) introduces a cooling note into an exuberant color scheme in which large orange squares alternately frame blue squares and squares-within-squares.

1 2 3 4 Pink Frames Soft plum pink in light (2) and medium (3) tones complement the bluish green (1). Neutral gray (4) isolates the green squares in the center of each block so they tend to recede. The pink frames, having a much brighter value than the other colors, takes center stage.

complementary/**Georgia**

Different emphases can be put on the very distinctive shapes that appear in repeated Georgia blocks by manipulating tones and colors. In **Regal Pomp** and **Pink Blossoms**, using paler fabrics in the center emphasizes a pattern of crosses, whereas in **Cloudy Octagons** and **Apple Green**, using lighter fabrics in the corners means that octagons dominate the design. Yet another effect appears in **Green Polka Dots**, when the darker colors form a background to the lighter ones.

 Regal Pomp Gold (1) and complementary purple (2) make a dazzling combination— a positively regal effect. This is slightly moderated by the pale oatmeal (3) patches in the center, positioned to reveal the pattern of crosses.

Rose Trellis Subdued background gray (1) is enlivened by the rosy pink (3) and contrasting olive (2), which form a pattern of squares and octagons in a gentle scheme evoking a rainy day in a summer garden.

Georgia template
This template shows the individual pieces of a block, irrespective of color.

Moorish Tiles The contrast between golden tan (2) and navy blue (1) is strong enough to reveal the pattern of octagons and squares, but it is the strategically placed bright blue (3) patches that give the quilt an extra twinkle, in a color scheme inspired by Moorish wall tiles.

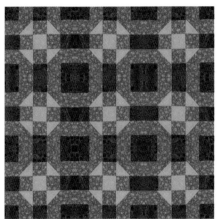

① ② ③ Cloudy Octagons Judiciously placed clover pink (3) injects a cheery note into an otherwise mild and subdued scheme dominated by the cloudy gray (2) octagons, alternating with sea green (1) squares.

① ② ③ Apple Green Palest apple green (2), dark olive (1), and pink (3) create a gentle, undemanding scheme with a warm heart. Ideal for situations where the quilt needs to blend into the décor rather than playing a starring part.

① ② ③ Green Polka Dots Very dark gray (1) and deep bluish purple (2) tend to merge to form a background to green (3) octagons that catch the eye and dominate the design, appearing almost like polka dots across the surface of the quilt.

① ② ③ Pink Blossoms Maroon (2) and a complementary green (1) give the square and rectangle shapes prominence, although the overall effect is quite subdued. The rosy pink (3), being of much lighter value than the other colors, adds a lighter note, like flowers among foliage.

complementary/**Grape Basket**

The color used for the large and smaller triangles determines the final effect for Grape Basket. In **Marigolds**, bright blue triangles resonate against the strong orange background, whereas in **Blue and Tan** the complementary colors are in the basket itself, so that it stands out more crisply against the background. **Good Vibrations** gains added drama when the complementary colors of the basket are set against a dark background.

1 2 3 **Marigolds** The combination of bright blue (3) and orange (1) could look a little too harsh, but the effect is mitigated by piecing the triangles round the edge of the basket in a floral print (2) that contains the other colors, but in more muted tones.

1 2 3 **Clover Field** The strongly contrasting deep pink (3) and green (2) of the basket are set into a paler version of pink (1), giving the quilt visual unity without detracting from the strong impact of the complementary colors.

Grape Basket template This template shows the individual pieces of a block, irrespective of color.

1 2 3 **Shoal of Goldfish** The outline triangles of the block are pieced in a medium purple print (2) so that when the basket is set in a dark purple (1) background the bright yellow (3) triangles stand out, suggesting fish shapes swimming across the surface.

1 2 3 **Blue and Tan** A simple but effective color scheme in which dark (3) and light blue (2) contrast with the bright tan (1) background. The dark blue triangles dominate the scheme because they contrast more strongly with the background.

1 2 3 **Blue Eyes** Bright Kingfisher blue (3) and contrasting brown (2) are set into a neutral blue-gray (1) background for a fresh, crisp looking quilt, although the background, echoing the blue, softens the effect.

1 2 3 **Basket of Olives** The shapes within the basket tend to blend together because they are pieced from light (3) and dark (2) shades of olive, but when set into deep midnight blue (1) they gain greater impact.

1 2 3 **Good Vibrations** Strong fuchsia pink (3) and bright green (2) make a strong visual impact and look even more dramatic when they are set against very dark gray (1) in a strong and assertive color scheme.

complementary/**Bear's Paw**

Whether you choose rich and dramatic colors, as in **Turquoise Points** and **Colors of the Indus,** or the cooler, fresher tones of **Plum Tree** and **Primrose Paths,** repeated Bear's Paw blocks make an interesting and complex quilt. In **Classic Red and Green** the complementary red and green make their usual impact, but the whole scheme is given a clean, fresh look by the addition of palest yellow.

1 **Field of Gold** The rich gold (1) provides a
2 background to the purple (2) of the grid, while
3 bright green (3) adds a gem-like touch to the sumptuous, glowing quilt. The colors are of a similar tone so elements of the pattern have equal visual impact.

1 **Turquoise Points** Tomato red (2) set
2 against a background of rusty black (1) looks
3 rich and glowing, while the subtly brighter value of aqua (3) adds a series of brilliant focal points and a little drama to the scheme.

Bear's Paw template
This template shows the individual pieces of a block, irrespective of color.

1 **Plum Tree** Soft plum (1) and its opposite
2 on the color wheel, lime green (3), are set
3 beneath a neutral grid in a much lighter value of the green (2), which gives the frames around the shapes the greatest impact and casts quite a cool effect over the whole surface.

1 **Arabian Nights** Colors inspired by those
2 seen in Moorish tile decorations are of similar
3 tones, but the mustard (2) is just a little
brighter than the soft midnight blue (1) and
dark olive green (3), so imparting a lighter
note to a quilt that might otherwise seem a
little somber.

1 **Classic Red and Green** Traditionally
2 quilters exploited the vibrant combination of
3 red (3) and green (2) complementary colors
by setting them in lighter backgrounds. In
this case, a very pale yellow (1) is used for
maximum impact.

1 **Primrose Paths** Blue (1) and tan (3),
2 highlighted by a grid of pale primrose (2),
3 make a color scheme that is fresh and crisp
without any hint of prettiness. The lighter tone
of the yellow ensures that the grid pattern
dominates the design.

1 **Colors of the Indus** A sumptuous
2 combination of colors inspired by Indian
3 textiles, in which muted gold (2) contrasts
strongly with deep purple (3) but less so with
the rusty red (1), slightly subduing an
otherwise exuberant color scheme.

complementary/**Lincoln's Platform**

Lincoln's Platform can be seen as a quick way of piecing a design of Churn Dash blocks set with sashings and posts. In **Pale Sashes**, this effect is emphasized as the very pale yellow used for the long patches contrasts strongly with the other two, complementary, colors. In **Green Islands** the purple and complementary green have equal value and the scheme is unified by the fact that the pale yellow contains a hint of green.

 Fuchsia Pink Dark (2) and light (3) tones of strong fuchsia pink are set against complementary aqua (1). Using the paler color for the grid introduces a slightly calmer atmosphere without detracting too much from the lively effect of the complementary colors.

Lincoln's Platform template This template shows the individual pieces of a block, irrespective of color.

1 2 3 Blue Windows Pale blue shapes (2), set against orange (1), appear behind the deep blue (3) windows created by the grid, but the contrast between the deep blue and orange has the major impact on the design, highlighting the orange "posts" where the lines of the grid meet.

1 2 3 Bands of Green The complementary pink (2) and green (3) are separated by deep blue (1), but since the larger proportion of the block is pieced in pink, the complementary colors still resonate and the blue recedes into the background. The green, lying over the other colors, gives a fresh, lively look.

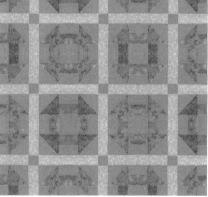

①
②
③
Midas Touch Gold (3) bands lying over dark (1) and light (2) tones of purplish blue contribute a suggestion of opulence to the more subdued effect created by the blues.

1
2
3
Green Islands Although the complementary olive (2) and purple (3) are separated by pale yellow (1), they are still attracted to each other, the yellow acting as a foil to the more definite colors.

①
②
3
Pale Sashes Delphinium blue (1) and complementary nut brown (2) are dynamic enough to stand up to the strong contrast of the neutral pale cream (3) grid in a fresh, lively color scheme.

①
②
③
Sweet Dianthus A quilt inspired by the colors of garden pinks (2), with their leaves in dark (1) and light (3) tones of green. The similar tones of pink and green between the frames give the shapes equal value, while the pale green frames give the whole surface a light, crisp effect.

complementary/**Claws**

Emphasis is given to different elements of the pattern, most notably the stars, by changing the positions of the complementary colors. In **Green Twinkle** the green stars seem especially bright set against red, the pale points adding to the generally clear and crisp design. In **Lost Points** the orange corner patches gain in importance by being juxtaposed with the complementary purplish background, whereas you have to look hard to see the star points, pieced in a dark tone of the purple.

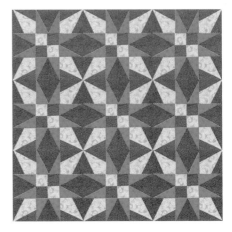

1 **2** **3** **Evening Stars** Soft tones of complementary yellow (3) and medium (1) and pale (2) lilac make a soothing quilt design in which the stars shine without dazzling.

1 **2** **3** **Green Twinkle** Green (3) stars twinkle out brightly from the red (1) background, while the very pale lilac (2) corner points enhance the generally fresh, crisp look of the quilt.

Claws template
This template shows the individual pieces of a block, irrespective of color.

1 **2** **3** **Amber Lights** Strong contrast between the amber (2) corner patches and the very deep midnight blue (1) of the background gives them dominance in the design. The lighter blue (3) of the stars means that they play a more subtle role in this dramatic color scheme.

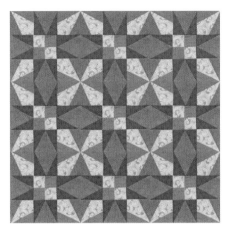

1 2 3 Lost Points The violet (3) points of the stars tend to merge into the bluish violet (1) background, while the corner points and squares in complementary soft orange (2) shine out against it, so that the shapes and patterns they form are the dominant elements of the design.

1 2 3 Fading Stars A subtle color scheme, emphasizing the four green (2) corner patches in each block, set against complementary deep pink (1). A hint of pink in the very dark gray (3) of the star points causes them to merge with the pink and fade into the background.

1 2 3 Bed of Violets A quilt with a gentle, floral theme. Soft violet (3) petals, surrounded by fresh green (2) leaves are set into a neutral background of palest gray (1), emphasizing both the stars and the other shapes between them.

1 2 3 Minton Tiles The colors and pattern in this example are typical of a classic Minton tile floor, the contrasting brown (1) and yellow (3) emphasizing the grid structure of the pattern, with the bright blue (2) contributing to a cheerful, practical color scheme.

complementary/**Puss in the Corner**

An illusion of diagonally set squares is created when complementary colors are juxtaposed to a third, strongly contrasting color, for example in **Black and Blue** and **Emerald Cloth**. A more cohesive effect is achieved when a simple combination of two complementary colors is used, as in **Square Dance** and **Raspberry Ripple**.

 Square Dance Speedwell blue (2) and two prints in which yellow (1, 3) predominates clearly reveal the basic structure of the design as squares and crosses because the yellows tend to merge into a single shape.

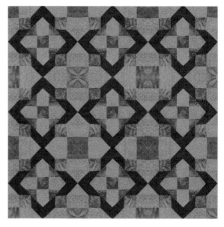

1 **Arrowheads** Bright candy pink (3) contrasts
2 well with complementary olive (2), but the
3 introduction of the much paler olive (1) interrupts the pink patches so they appear as individual shapes, resembling arrowheads, across the surface of the quilt.

Puss in the Corner template This template shows the individual pieces of a block, irrespective of color.

1 **Black and Blue** Tawny brown (1) is
2 complementary to bright kingfisher blue (2),
3 but the black (3) in the long patches immediately grabs the eye, outlining a series of squares and crosses across the surface. A strong, effective color scheme, the black adding a touch of drama to it.

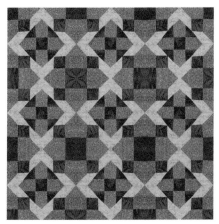

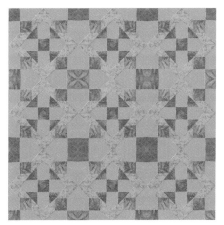

1 **2** **3** **Emerald Cloth** Emerald green (2) makes a vivid background to the complementary chocolate-brown (1) shapes, while the long, gray (3) shapes seem to hover below the brown squares that lie on the green background.

1 **2** **3** **Bronze Glow** A quilt in dignified Victorian style, in which rich bronze (2) contrasts with plum purple (1), and a pattern of pale lilac (3) squares add a little light relief without detracting from the generally rich overall effect.

1 **2** **3** **Floating Squares** Pale pinkish-gray (1) shapes seem to float ethereally over the strong underlying pattern created by juxtaposing rose pink (3) and complementary olive green (2), although the pink squares make the major contribution to the scheme.

1 **2** **3** **Raspberry Ripple** A subtle distinction between soft raspberry pink (1) and a slightly paler version (3) defines the pattern of squares and triangles that ripples over the pretty, mint green (2) of the background in a dainty, feminine color scheme.

complementary/**Star of the East**

Stars can be pieced from two complementary colors, as seen in **Complementary Stars** and **Green Highlights**, when a dark background tends to produce a rich, somber effect, or in **Sunset Sky**, when a light background gives a more lighthearted atmosphere. When, as in **Parma Violets** and **Skylights**, two shades of the same color are used for the stars, using a complementary color for the background gives the stars heightened definition and the three-dimensional effect is more marked.

Green Highlights Stars pieced in brilliant acid green (2) and a darker, more sober tone of complementary red (3) are set into a textured gray, black, and gold print (1) background. Because there is less contrast between the two darker colors, the green tends to dominate the scheme.

Aquamarine Perspectives Soft, warm tomato red (1) for the background makes a perfect foil for the cool, faceted stars pieced in dark (2) and light (3) tones of complementary aquamarine, while at the same time imparting a slightly subtle and subdued note to the scheme.

Parma Violets Two tones of violet, light (2) and medium (3), are well defined against a medium leaf green (1), which, however, is just dark enough in tone to avoid mere prettiness in a charming quilt with a floral theme.

Star of the East template This template shows the individual pieces of a block, irrespective of color.

1 2 3 **Sunset Sky** The sweet pink (1) background, while acting almost as a neutral, still unifies the scheme while allowing the more assertive darker pink (2) and green (3) of the stars to stand out and set the tone.

1 2 3 **Skylights** Three-dimensional stars in orange (2) and yellow (3) sparkle out from a deep, midnight blue (1) sky in a classic color scheme that never fails to promote a cheerful, optimistic mood.

1 2 3 **Complementary Stars** Complementary pinkish red (3) and green (2) gain added intensity when set into a deep gray (1) background, but the greatest contrast is between the background and the red, so it is the red that appears to be the brightest and most dominant color in the scheme.

1 2 3 **Sea of Stars** A sophisticated color scheme in which the main effect is achieved through the contrast between the cool sea greens (2, 3) of the stars and the warm, dark pink (1) of the background, the faceted quality of the stars adding to the general brightness and intensity of the design.

EIGHT-POINTED STARS

complementary/**Virginia Star**

Strong contrast between the outer diamonds of the star and the background emphasize the linear elements that appear in repeated blocks of Virginia Star, an effect seen most clearly in **Elegant Star** and **Center Stage**. When, as in **Wildflower Meadow** and **Sunsplash**, there is less contrast, the diamonds tend to disappear into the background so that the stars appear more isolated.

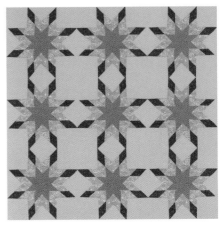

①②③④ Celebration Quilt Bright, clear red (1) and green (2) echo colors in the floral print (3) for a cheerful quilt in traditional Christmas colors. The dark patterned fabric (4) in the center of the stars makes a dramatic focus.

①②③④ Fruit Fool Blackcurrant (2) diamonds give the stars definition against the pale orange (1) background, while the design is unified by placing the stronger orange (4) in the center of the stars, where it gains added intensity from being placed against the paler blackcurrant (3).

①②③④ Sunsplash Two tones of lemon yellow (3, 4) merge to make a splash against the complementary magenta (1), but the discreet introduction of the more subdued olive (2) diamonds at the tips of the stars slightly softens the effect.

Virginia Star template
This template shows the individual pieces of a block, irrespective of color.

1 **Wildflower Meadow** Grass green (1)
2 makes a carpet for starry flowers pieced in
3 dark (3) and medium (4) violet, the olive (2)
4 diamonds fading gently into the background
to soften the contrast between the
complementary colors.

1 **Warm Hearts** Deep brownish pink (1) lends
2 a warm glow to the vibrant aquamarine stars
3 (2, 3) while the deep pink (4) centers, echoing
4 the background, bring the design together
without detracting from the visual impact of
the stars.

1 **Elegant Star** A simple contrast between
2 complementary colors, using deep and pale
3 tones of both blue (2, 3) and lemon yellow
4 (1, 4) emphasize the formal, linear design of
repeated blocks in a refined and elegant quilt.

1 **Center Stage** Brick red (3) and
2 complementary mid-aqua (4) have the
3 greatest visual impact and take center stage.
4 Pale blue (2) diamonds at the tips of the
stars, placed against the dark gray (1)
background, serve to highlight the square
and diamond shapes in the background.

complementary/**Bow Tie**

Vary the tone and intensity of complementary colors to achieve startlingly different results from one simple pattern. Bronze and jade are used to capture the feel of classic quilts in **Antique Quilt**, or you can go for the really sparkling effects of the blues and oranges used in **Kids' Room**. With its clear contrasts emphasized by judicious touches of black, **Spick-and-Span** looks smart and clean-cut.

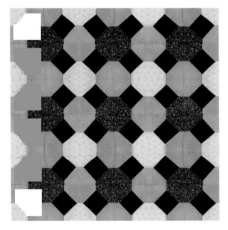

①②③④ **Spick-and-Span** Lively contrast between bright lime green (3) and red (4) can't fail to make an impact, and when black (2) adds a dramatic touch, and yellow (1) a series of bright spots, the result is a clean-cut, vibrant quilt, which would look great in a boy's room.

①②③④ **Double Pinks** When two tones of pink, deep (1) and pale (4), are juxtaposed to their opposites on the color wheel, medium (2) and pale (3) aqua, the result is a light, pretty quilt in which the slightly brighter tones of the two pinks tend to predominate.

①②③④ **Plum Pies** Cool/warm contrast between deep olive (3) and complementary plum (4) lends this quilt depth; the addition of charcoal gray (1) could give a rather somber effect, but the introduction of the very pale version of the green (2) lightens and brightens the whole mood.

Bow Tie template
This template shows the individual pieces of a block, irrespective of color.

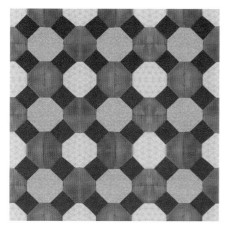

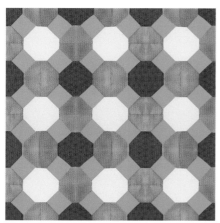

①②③④ Cyclamen Squares Mid-olive (3) octagons seem to lie at the intersections of a connecting pattern of cyclamen pink (2) squares surrounding paler green (1) and pink (4) octagons, emphasizing the brighter elements of the design.

①②③④ Winter Hellebores Sky blue (2) and a hint of green in the bright yellow (4) evoke the colors of hellebores appearing on a fine, late winter's day. Navy blue (1) and olive (3) add a suitably subduing note to an otherwise cheerful, practical quilt.

①②③④ Antique Quilt Jade green (2), antique bronze (3), and mahogany (4) set the tone for a quilt with a classic nineteenth-century look. Contrast between the green and orange gives a little vibrancy to the pattern, while the neutral grayish green (1) gives the scheme a necessary lift.

①②③④ Kids' Room Alternating complementaries, mauve (1) and sunshine yellow (3), and azure blue (4) and bright orange (2), give this quilt a real zing, the slightly muted tone of the mauve serving to calm it down—but not too much! A great quilt for a child's room.

complementary/**Kaleidoscope**

The visual impact of complementary colors can be exaggerated or modified according to the surrounding colors and tones. Kaleidoscope, with its capacity for optical illusion, illustrates this perfectly. In **Turning Puce** and **Kaleidoscope Classic**, all the fabrics are of similar tone, so multiplying the combinations that the eye can pick out: four-pointed stars with squares at the centers, or a series of interlocking circles. In **Primrose Lights** the brighter tone used to separate the shapes gives the long diamonds prominence.

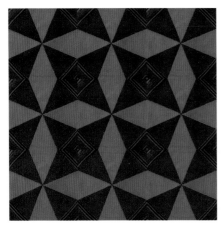

❶ ❷ ❸ Kaleidoscope Classic Although used in slightly somber tones, nut brown (2) and complementary turquoise (3), both echoed in the striped print (1) used for the corner triangles, still have impact as they reveal the ambiguity of a pattern that can be read in several ways.

❶ ❷ ❸ Turning Puce Ash gray (1) corners join as squares to contribute subtle "punctuation marks" in the main patterns formed by puce (2) triangles and complementary green (3) diamonds, in which the puce triangles can seem to join as circles, or, alternatively, to form four-pointed stars set in green octagons.

1 2 3 Primrose Lights A very pale primrose yellow (1) is juxtaposed to blue (2) in a much darker tone, so that although proportionally less in the whole design it imparts a generally clear, bright atmosphere because it contrasts strongly with the more somber contributions of the blue and olive (3).

Kaleidoscope template
This template shows the individual pieces of a block, irrespective of color.

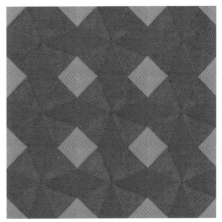

1 2 3 **Amethyst Diamond** Alternating dark (2) and light (3) tones of amethyst combine in a classic kaleidoscope quilt, with complementary olive green (1) triangles separating and defining the main shapes. The diamond shapes in the lighter amethyst, being brighter than the other fabrics, catch the eye first.

1 2 3 **Bronze Sheen** Subdued tones of pine green (2) and bronze (3) combine in a quilt with muted resonance. The brighter tone of the bronze gives the long diamonds immediate impact, while nut brown (1) contributes low-key definition to the surrounding shapes.

1 2 3 **Calming Touch** A soft tone of rusty orange (2) set against a brighter tone of complementary blue (3) looks bold and lively, but the use of soft, slate gray (1) between the other shapes has a calming influence and makes the quilt easier on the eye.

1 2 3 **Scarlet Pimpernel** Green (1) and scarlet (2) always produce resonance, so the eye is drawn to the four-pointed stars within green centers. Gray (3) diamonds tend to recede slightly behind the other shapes, serving to reduce the slightly glaring effect that bright reds and greens can sometimes produce.

complementary/**Lattice and Square**

The squares made by the long rectangle patches naturally tend to come forward and dominate the design, especially when, as in **Exotic Aura** and **In the Purple**, they are pieced in a significantly brighter tone than the other shapes. Notice, though, that in **Chain Links**, where all the fabrics are of similar tone, the pattern is more ambiguous and difficult to read.

❶ ❷ ❸ Exotic Aura There is a distinctly exotic aura to this combination of blood red (1) and jade green (3), and the scheme gains even greater depth and richness when indigo blue (2) is added. The brighter tone of the green squares-on-point makes the shapes formed by them the main focus.

Lattice and Square template This template shows the individual pieces of a block, irrespective of color.

❶ ❷ ❸ Cornerstones Blue (3) windows stand out well from a background of complementary amber (1). However, the brighter tone of the small, stone (2) squares means that they also make their mark, so the blue squares can also be seen to alternate with amber crosses with stone corner squares.

❶ ❷ ❸ Garden Borders A striking yet practical combination in which squares of earthy brown (1) are bordered by bright grassy green (3) squares, alternating with brown crosses with light olive (2) cornerposts.

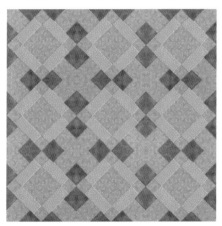

①②③ Chain Links The colors here have been used in similar tones, resulting in a degree of ambiguity in reading the pattern; amber (1) crosses with green (2) corners can be picked out, but the blue (3) squares, rather than standing out as isolated shapes, appear to be linked across the surface to the other shapes.

①②③ Pink Charm A gentle, charming quilt that avoids being merely pretty when soft pink (1), proportionately greater over the quilt surface, is broken up by complementary green (3) windows and small squares of a soft, smoky gray (2).

①②③ Emerald Squares The strongest contrast here is between sugar pink (1) and dark emerald (2), so the cranberry (3) shapes assume less importance than they might otherwise have, while the shapes formed where the green squares and sugar pink meet gain added definition.

①②③ In the Purple Gold squares (3) on majestic purple (1) have to take center stage, the squares in very dark green (2) making only shadowy appearances but serving to slightly mitigate the immediate impact of the contrast between the two main colors.

complementary/**Washington Pavement**

The corner squares can be used to influence the mood created by complementary colors in the centers of the blocks, so although those in **Lavender Parterre**, for example, are very effective on their own, the addition of gray confirms a generally calm, restrained effect, while in **Three Deep**, black imparts a positively dramatic influence over the whole design. A light, crisp look is achieved in **Jade Ribbons** by juxtaposing strong center colors to neutral corners.

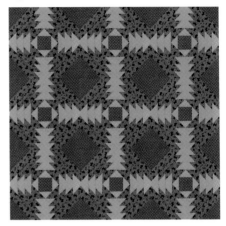

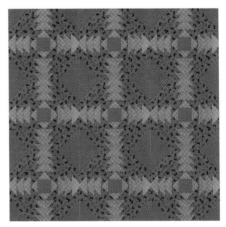

1 **2** **3** **Three Deep** Black (1) imparts a distinctly dramatic look at it throws up the contrast between the blue (2) and the golden yellow prints (3), at the same time emphasizing the illusion of layers in which the black lies under blue squares topped by a grid formed by the yellow triangles.

Washington Pavement template This template shows the individual pieces of a block, irrespective of color.

1 **2** **3** **Blue Feathers** Donkey brown (1) corners form on-point squares that recede within the fudge brown (2) squares around them, leaving the pattern formed by the bright blue (3) triangles to shine out as the main focus

1 **2** **3** **Lavender Parterre** The contrast between medium lavender (2) and complementary jade green (3) is understated when both are used in subdued tones, the slightly hazy overall effect being enforced by the addition of slate gray (1) in the corners, although the pattern formed by green triangles still catches the eye.

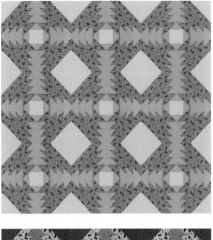

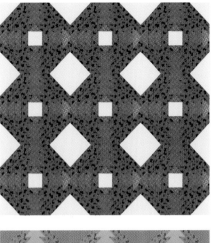

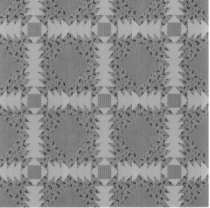

①②③ Jade Ribbons The juxtaposition of pinkish red (2) squares-on-point, overlaid by a network of jade green (3) triangles, gives a bold pattern of octagons crossed by jade squares. When these are set against a neutral background in greenish cream (1), the effect is a pleasingly light and summery quilt.

①②③ Midnight Garden Deep midnight purple (1) squares seem to lie under octagons of yellowish lime-green (2) in a brighter tone, in turn overlaid by a network of lilac (3) triangles, which has the effect of restraining the underlying lime shapes.

①②③ Graphic Impact A strong design in which octagons in slightly dull tones of blue (2) and tan (3) are given maximum definition when they are set off against a background of cream (1) squares in a much brighter shade, so the final effect is surprisingly clean-cut and fresh.

①②③ Lightning Touch Squares of pale dove gray (1) have a calming effect on this combination of soft rusty red (2) and brighter medium aqua (3), which contributes flashes of bright color across the surface of an otherwise gentle and restrained scheme.

complementary/**Winding Ways**

With just two fabrics, the pattern's main impact comes from the alternation between negative and positive shapes. In **Razzle Dazzle**, strong tones of colors exactly opposite each other on the color wheel emphasize this effect, while in **Soft and Muted**, although the colors are complementary, they are used in such subdued tones that the effect is soothing, not assertive. In **Blue Sky and Sunshine**, sky blue is used with yellow, which, being next to blue's complementary, orange, on the color wheel gives strong visual contrast.

❶
❷ **Bright and Cool** Red (1) and green (2), as opposites on the color wheel, lend visual intensity to each other. This red, which contains a hint of violet, makes the yellow-green next to it appear brighter and cooler than it might otherwise seem.

Winding Ways template
This template shows the individual pieces of a block, irrespective of color.

❶
❷ **Blue Sky and Sunshine** Sky blue (1) and yellow (2) create a lively, optimistic mood echoing the colors of blue sky and sunshine. Although the brighter tone of the yellow tends to make it come forward, the blue is strong enough to stand up to it and the shapes in both colors vie for attention.

❶
❷ **Good Vibrations** Strong shades of complementary purple (2) and orange (1) create an optical vibration when placed together, giving a strong and eye-catching color scheme—perfect for a wake-me-up-in-the-morning quilt.

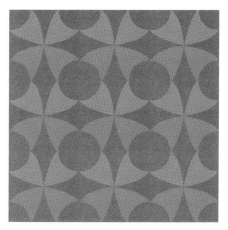

1
2 **Razzle Dazzle** A really dazzling color scheme. Bright ruby red (2) and an equally strong sea green (1), compete for attention where they meet. This has the effect of confusing the eye, so that one is constantly trying to decide which color and shapes are dominant.

1
2 **Cool and Warm** Tints of minty green (2) and dusky pink (1) look cool and pretty but have sufficient contrast to define the pattern. Pink is usually perceived as a warm color but the muted tint used here reduces that effect.

1
2 **Chocolate and Lime** The rich brown (1) is a foil for the zingy lime green (2), which might otherwise appear hard on the eye. This is a color scheme to create a strong dynamic-looking quilt.

1
2 **Soft and Muted** Surprisingly, these fabrics are the classic complementaries, red (1) and green (2), although both colors contain a hint of blue and are muted by the addition of gray. The subtle contrast is sufficient to play the colors off against each other and give the pattern definition.

complementary/**Round Table**

Using complementary colors with counterchange patterns like Round Table, where negative and positive shapes and colors are juxtaposed, can create stunning effects. While the center circles could be seen simply as "punctuation marks," they can actually influence the whole design quite strongly. In **Chocolate Buttons** and **Beach Balls**, for instance, the addition of the center circle in a slightly duller tone adds a necessary sobering touch, while in **Moonlit Garden** the center circles act as strong focal points.

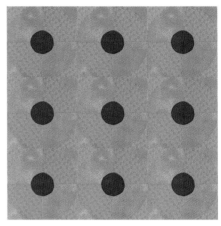

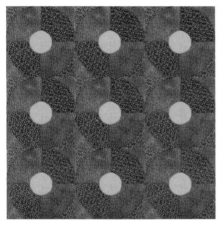

1 2 3 Gold Rings Cherry red (1) and a complementary emerald green (2) make their usual impact, and the lively, vibrant character of the quilt is enhanced by gold (3) circles, for a reassuringly traditional ambience.

1 2 3 Chocolate Buttons Ultramarine (1) and complementary marmalade orange (2) contrast brilliantly, with all elements of the pattern well defined. The chocolate (3) circles seem like a series of evenly placed buttons, contributing understated focal points without detracting from the clean-cut overall effect.

1 2 3 Gray Eyes The slightly subdued impression made by combining softened tones of emerald green (1) and rosy pink (2) is underscored by the pale, pearly gray (3) center circles, so the final effect is quite gentle and restrained.

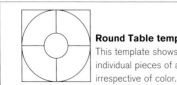

Round Table template
This template shows the individual pieces of a block, irrespective of color.

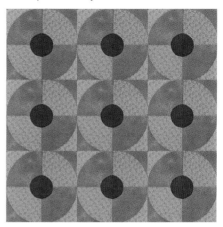

①②③ Bowling Along The vibrant, cheerful impact of indigo blue (1) juxtaposed to sunny yellow (2) is even greater when dark/light contrast between them is heightened. Neutral cream (3) "buttons," toning with the yellow, serve to ensure that the quilt isn't dominated by the blue.

①②③ Olive Pips The effect of a strong contrast between bright lime green (1) and a darker tone of lavender (2) is slightly modified by the introduction of dark olive (3) circles, imparting a tranquil atmosphere to the whole scheme.

①②③ Beach Balls A marriage of mid-aqua (1) and complementary bright tomato red (2) has the exuberance of colorful beach balls, checked by the introduction of small charcoal gray (3) circles marking a series of slightly sobering focal points.

①②③ Moonlit Garden The main pattern is almost lost in very subdued contrast between dark tones of plum purple (1) and moss green (2), the purple shapes appearing as a series of "bows," so that the bright cream (3) circles steal the scene, shining out as a series of bright focal points.

complementary/**Japanese Fan**

When fans in the formal Japanese Fan pattern are pieced in complementary colors, the background then determines the overall mood and style, although a neutral background, as in **Rich and Dignified**, may simply be a foil for the main impression made by the fans. In **Fans to Go!**, the apricot is just strong enough to stand up against the more dynamic fans, so plays a central part in the overall effect, whereas in **Subtle Impact** the background is a foil to the fans, but serves to impart a lighter, brighter mood to the whole quilt.

1 **2** **3** **4** **Rich and Dignified** The strong impression made by gold (2) and a very dark, rich brown (3) is only slightly moderated by outlining the fans in rust (4). When set on a neutral coffee cream (1) background the effect is rather rich and dignified.

1 **2** **3** **4** **Subtle Impact** A bright, pale greenish yellow (1) background brightens and enhances the potentially somber effect of fans pieced in subdued tones of deep violet (2) and olive (3), a subtle combination underlined by deepest blackish green (4) used for the center circles and outlining strips.

1 **2** **3** **4** **Outward-looking** A sky blue (1) background and fans in gold (2) and indigo blue (3) combine to create a cheerful, optimistic mood, the fans gaining even more distinction when bright yellow (4) circles and rims are added.

Japanese Fan template
This template shows the individual pieces of a block, irrespective of color.

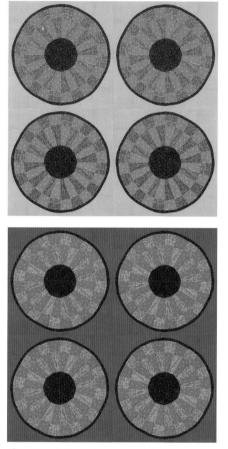

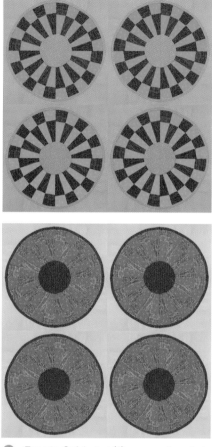

① **Electric Fans** A pearl gray (1) sky casts a
② calming light on fans pieced in burnt orange
③ (2) and complementary electric blue (3),
④ which might otherwise be a little hard on the
eye. Chocolate brown (4) for the center
circles and rims of the wheels adds a touch
of depth to the scheme.

① **Fans in the Forest** Jade green (2) and
② complementary soft pink (3) give the fans
③ modest vibrancy, emphasized by black (4) for
④ the center circles and outlining strips. Placed
on the dark forest green (1) background the
overall effect is quite dense and rich.

① **Fans to Go!** Apricot (1) can sometimes look
② a little understated and "safe," but used here
③ as a background it is the perfect foil for fans
④ pieced in dark brown (2) and bright sky blue
(3), which are only faintly outlined by deep
peach (4) centers and strips, resulting in a
lively, dynamic quilt.

① **Cooling Fans** In the fans, bluish green (2) is
② complemented by mulberry (3), a darker tone
③ of which (4) is used for the circles and outline
④ strips. When set on a background of icy blue
(1), which is a paler version of (2), contrast
between the cool blues and warmer pinks
makes for a striking quilt.

complementary/**Friendship Fan**

A scheme based on two main colors always makes a bold statement, but the choice of color and tone for the third ingredient, although proportionately a lesser element, is actually vital to the final effect. In **Brighter Focus**, for example, the main colors are quite rich and could be a little overpowering, so adding neutral cream circles lifts and brightens the whole mood. In **Lime Flavor**, a softer tone of brown moderates the contrast between the two complementary colors, without detracting from the overall effect.

① ② ③ Purple Rings Medium tones of lime green (1) and lilac (2) make a lively combination with a fresh, spring-like feel, only slightly modulated by the addition of dark purple (3) rings.

① ② ③ Brighter Focus High contrast between rich tones of purple (1) and amber (2) makes for a quilt with vivid impact, toned down just a little by a series of bright focal points provided by the neutral cream (3) rings.

Friendship Fan template This template shows the individual pieces of a block, irrespective of color.

① ② ③ Oriental Poppies Brilliant Shirley poppies in bright orange (1), seen against a perfect high-summer sky (2), inspired this vibrant scheme in which leaf green (3) circles contribute a small but important note to the garden theme.

❶
❷
❸
Lime Flavor Chocolate brown (1) and lime green (2) look smart and stylish together, although the green, proportionately greater in the design and in a brighter tone, imparts a very lively mood, just slightly moderated by the soft brown (3) circles.

❶
❷
❸
Variation on a Theme A subtle variation on the classic juxtaposition of complementary red and green gives a softer feel, while retaining a pleasing vibrancy, when emerald green (1) is used with a soft tone of rose pink (2), and the design is overlaid by rings in palest pearl gray (3).

❶
❷
❸
Leading Light Minty green (1) and pale shell pink (2) offer yet another variation on the traditional red/green theme, with the lighter tone of the pink giving it the main role in the design, an effect that is underscored when a deeper, duskier tone of the pink (3) appears in the circles.

❶
❷
❸
Sobering Influence Candy pink (1) and petrol blue (2) make for a dynamic quilt surface, although the deeper tone of the blue, matched with khaki (3) rings has a slightly sobering effect on the pink, so that the overall effect is quite rich.

When complementary colors appear in the circles and the petal shapes within them, those elements of the pattern naturally tend to dominate the eye, as you can see in both **Chocolate Limes** and **Bed of Violets**. You will also see, however, that the colors and tones used between the circles have a determining effect on the final outcome. For example, in **Bed of Violets** the dark shapes contribute a slightly dramatic note, and in **First Impressions** the light tone almost takes center stage.

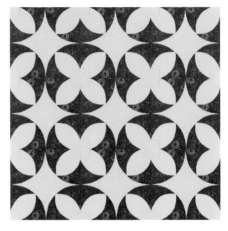

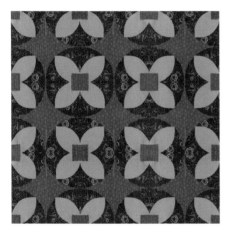

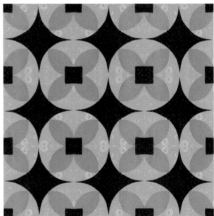

1 2 3 Classic Red and Green The combination of Turkey red (3) and green (1), beloved by so many nineteenth-century quilt-makers, never fails to impress. In this example the addition of old gold (2), while highlighting the center petal shapes, confirms the overall impression of a classic quilt in traditional style.

Bleeding Hearts template This template shows the individual pieces of a block, irrespective of color.

1 2 3 Chocolate Limes Strong contrast between bright lime (2) and dark chocolate brown (3) emphasizes the impression of light petals on dark circles, although the curve-sided shapes in pearl gray (1) also make an impact, resulting in an elegant, well-balanced design with a surprisingly airy feel to it.

1 2 3 Floating Petals Orange (2) petals lying on pools of complementary aqua (3) make a strong visual statement, reinforced by the addition of inky blue (1), which sharpens and defines the dominant shapes in a striking and unusual quilt design with just a touch of drama.

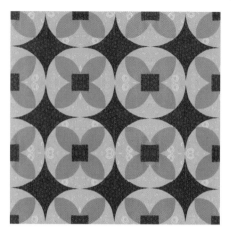

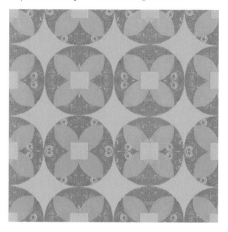

1 **Bed of Violets** Violet (2) petals are
2 surrounded by a light tone of complementary
3 spring green (3), a combination that could
look merely pretty, but strong contrast
between those colors and dark charcoal gray
(1) gives the main shapes full value and
results in a strong, well-balanced design.

1 **First Impressions** By using the neutral
2 coffee cream (1) as background, the curve-
3 sided shapes come forward strongly and
make the first impression on the eye, despite
the fact that the blue (3) and complementary
tan (2) also make a strong statement. The
result is a fascinatingly complex quilt design.

1 **Balancing Act** Similar tones of blue (3) and
2 complementary apricot (2) are well matched
3 by pretty apple green (1), so that all the
shapes have definition and compete for
attention, the overall effect being both
complex and pleasingly well-balanced.

1 **Early Primroses** Violet (2) petal shapes on
2 complementary olive (3) make a strong
3 statement, but when the circles are separated
by pale primrose (1), those are the shapes
that come forward and catch the eye, so that
the final effect is generally rather lighthearted
and spring-like.

The shapes made by the tulips' flower heads in repeated blocks are often the least obvious elements of the design, because the leaf and stem shapes and the center circles join to form such a distinctive pattern. In **Fuchsia Elegans** and **Fading Flowers**, for example, the tulips recede to become part of a background for the brighter flower shapes. On the other hand, when contrast between the tulip heads and the background is very strong, they hold their own in the design, as you can see in **Victorian Plush** and **Floral Print**.

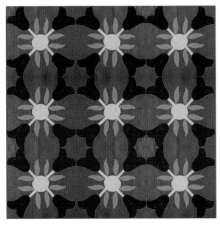

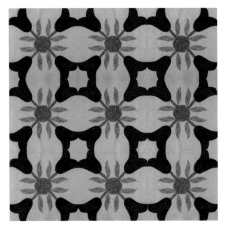

(1) (2) (3) (4) Victorian Plush Deep aubergine (2) juxtaposed to complementary antique gold (1) always looks sumptuous, an impression confirmed here by the addition of a touch of gem-like green (3) leaves and dark mauve (4) for the stems and centers.

(1) (2) (3) (4) Fuchsia Elegans A quilt inspired by the purply red flowers (2) of fuchsias offset by their leaves in complementary bottle green (1), which tend to recede behind the shapes made by the bluish-green (3) used for the leaf shapes and pale sage (4) stems and centers, which make the main impression.

(1) (2) (3) (4) Shocking Pink Shocking pink (2) and complementary green (3) used for the leaves can't fail to make a dramatic impact when set on a black (1) background, the yellow (4) stems and center circle adding a light, bright touch in a series of focal points.

Dutch Tulips template
This template shows the individual pieces of a block, irrespective of color.

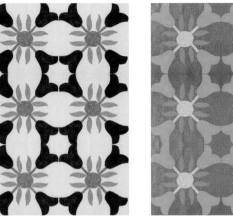
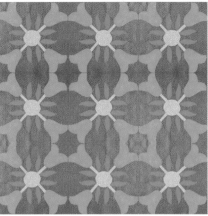

1 2 3 4 **Floral Print** Strong contrast between creamy yellow (1) and much darker complementary blue (2) gives strong definition to the square shapes made by the tulip heads, which vie for attention with the florets made by blue-green (3) leaves and orange (4) stems and centers in a well-balanced, fresh-looking quilt.

1 2 3 4 **Daisy Chains** Green (2) tulip heads show up well on the complementary burnt ginger (1) background, but the very pale green (3) and dark forest green (4) used for the leaves, stems, and centers outshine both complementary colors, and show as daisy-like shapes on top of the underlying pattern.

1 2 3 4 **Fading Flowers** Two complementaries used in soft, understated tones, lilac (1) and green (2), tend to fade behind brighter tones of green (3) and pink (4), the pale pink in the centers being just bright enough to give some focus to the design without detracting from the generally gentle, relaxing overall effect.

1 2 3 4 **Cornflowers** Although shapes made by the purple (2) of the tulip heads show up strongly against the neutral cream (1) of the background, the flower-like shapes made by navy blue (3) leaves and electric blue (4) stems and centers compete for attention and inject a cheery, lively note into the design.

Saturated
Colors

Saturated colors are
pure, deep-dyed colors,
often described as "intense."
Intensity is the relative degree to
which a color is pure—that is, free of
mixture with white, black, or gray. Intense
colors have special characteristics of depth and
richness, and so are perfect for creating dense, glowing
quilts. Both the Amish and Welsh quiltmakers have a strong
tradition of quilts that utilize large areas of saturated colors,
resulting in characteristically bold and striking quilts.
Intense colors can be mixed with a range of other tones
and values to give them added impact, but care
must be taken to get the mixture just right.
When two saturated colors are used
together, the overall effect can be
toned down a little by
juxtaposing other, less
intense, colors.

saturated/**Cross and Square**

Some surprising effects appear when saturated colors dominate the scheme, but because they tend to be of similar tones, it is often a good idea to marry them with significantly darker or lighter tones. In **Cappuccino Stars**, for example, a pale coffee color has been introduced as a main player, so the stars and the linear dimensions of the pattern stand out. In **Victoriana** a smaller proportion of black adds definition to certain elements of the pattern without dominating it.

❶
❷
❸
Goldmine A rich and glowing scheme based on a red fabric (1) overprinted with intense greens and gold, which have been picked up in the supporting colors. The deep gold (3) forms a background to the deep, cool turquoise (2) stars, which provide welcome contrast to the hotter, more vibrant colors.

❶
❷
❸
Exotic Magenta Exotic magenta (1) sets the tone, while tan brown (2) and green (3) combine to act as a foil to the more intense and vibrant color. Both the brown and green have a slightly yellowish tinge so that they blend together and the stars almost vanish.

❶
❷
❸
Deep-dyed Stars Contrast between the deep leafy green (3) and bark brown (1) is understated, so that they form a background to the deep-dyed blue (2) of the stars, an unusual combination resulting in a subtle and sophisticated color scheme.

Cross and Square template This template shows the individual pieces of a block, irrespective of color.

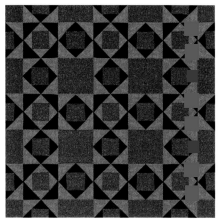

1 2 3 Set Square Deep lilac (2) tends to get lost against the purplish blue (3), so leaving golden brown (1) to make the major impact, the pattern showing as a series of squares rather than stars at first glance.

1 2 3 Cappuccino Stars Two intense colors, reddish purple (1) and dark chocolate brown (3), are set off by the much paler, contrasting coffee (2), which highlights the pattern of linked stars and the linear shape of the design, viewed both laterally and diagonally.

1 2 3 Mondrian Deep-dyed purple (3) is matched with an even darker slate blue (2) so the patches merge to form single shapes. The shapes resemble a pattern of lines on a bright turquoise (1) background, producing a quilt surface with pronounced linear movement echoing the paintings of Mondrian.

1 2 3 Victoriana Black (3), a strong feature of Victorian decoration, imparts calmness and structure to any color scheme. In this example, it emphasizes the formal structure of the design and contrasts beautifully with the plush damask pink (1) and toning slate blue (2).

saturated/**Amish Style**

Saturated colors tend to be of similar tones, so it's important to include fabrics that provide variation in tone to highlight different elements of the pattern. This is achieved in **Classic Amish**, where a flash of red creates highlights, while in **Glowing Amber** black is used to impart a jewel-like intensity to the other colors. **Pink Squares** illustrates the influence that discreet use of a neutral color can have on the final effect.

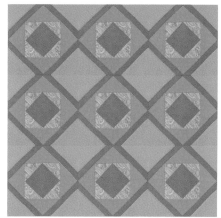

Glowing Amber Glowing amber (1) is echoed in the print fabric (4) used round the center squares, giving the quilt a sense of unity and balance. Vivid turquoise (2) gives strong definition to the pattern and the black (3) adds depth and intensity to a generally strong and assertive scheme.

Amish Style template
This template shows the individual pieces of a block, irrespective of color.

Harmony and Contrast Reddish brown (1) and poster red (2) make a harmonious combination that is enlivened by the strongly contrasting mid-aqua (3). A slightly muted tone of yellow (4) separates the brighter colors and serves to emphasize contrasts in a quilt with a bright, warm feel to it.

Pink Squares There is a pleasing contrast between the two cool colors, mid-aqua (1) and green (3), and warm pink (2). Using pale coffee (4) as a neutral to surround the pink center squares gives them the main role in the design and emphasizes the effect of alternating squares-on-point.

1 **Classic Amish** A characteristically Amish
2 selection of intense colors. Deep blue (2) and
3 brown (3) are of a similar tone but the bright
4 red (4) creates vibrant highlights. Subdued
contrast between the blue used to outline the
pieced squares and the black (1) backgound
confirms a rich, dense overall effect.

1 **Jewel Box Quilt** Deep blue (1) and mid-aqua
2 (2) look cool and harmonious together but the
3 whole scheme is lifted by the addition of the
4 old gold (4). Juxtaposing black (3) to gold and
aqua adds definition to the shapes and lends a
jewel-like quality to the other colors.

1 **Hot and Cold** Bright tones of hot red (1) and
2 cool, complementary jade green (3) give
3 a dynamic feel to this quilt, slightly moderated
4 by adding intense blue (2) to harmonize with
the green. A touch of purple (4) round the
center squares provides contrast and adds
complexity to the scheme.

1 **Purple Field** Another authentic Amish color
2 scheme in which the juxtaposition of electric
3 blue (2) to bright red (4) in the center creates
4 a vibrant focal point, which appears even
more brilliant when surrounded by black (3).
A purple (1) background to the squares-on-
point enhances the rich overall effect.

saturated/**Georgia**

When three squares in the center of Georgia are pieced in the same color some interesting graphic effects are seen. Sometimes, as in **Chinese Lanterns** and **Vertical Lines**, the design is dominated by the vertical elements, whereas in **Octagon Blues**, for example, the vibration between the two main colors is so strong that it commands the most attention and the other colors sinks into the background.

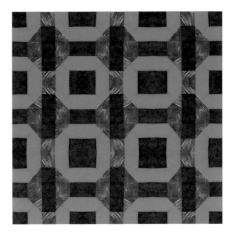

❶❷❸ Octagon Blues A pattern of bright electric blue (2) octagons, enclosing pink (1) squares, is seen. Strong contrast between the blue, which has a touch of green, and the complementary intense pink creates a very dynamic scheme, slightly moderated by the swirly print (3).

Georgia template
This template shows the individual pieces of a block, irrespective of color.

❶❷❸ Chinese Lanterns Triangles and squares pieced in bright tomato red (3), positioned around the rectangles formed by squares pieced in indigo blue (1), look like lanterns shining out from the surrounding blue and green (2). A quilt with a very unusual and contemporary looking design.

❶❷❸ Mulberries A pattern of large mulberry pink (2) octagons dominates the design, interspersed with small blue (3) octagons. The very deep mulberry (1) patches are seen as both squares and rectangles lying across the octagons, emphasizing the mosaic quality of the pattern.

① ② ③ **Fall Leaves** There is a hint of fall in the dark olive green (1) and soft brown (3), which merge together to form a backdrop to the more dramatic tone of the intense cyclamen pink (2) octagons.

① ② ③ **Red Rings** Complementary red (2) and green (1) ensure that the red octagons surrounding green squares have maximum impact, while the bright blue (3) adds a vibrant touch without being too intrusive.

① ② ③ **Vertical Lines** Cool, neutral gray (3) softens the bright gold (1) and donkey brown (2), at the same time placing emphasis on the pattern of vertical stripes so that brown octagons tend to recede. Another "lanterns" pattern (see Chinese Lanterns) with a distinctly contemporary look.

① ② ③ **Old Gold** Saturated colors are used to create a quilt with a consciously antique look to it. Old gold (2) octagons, in an intense tone, are matched with complementary purple (1), while the small rusty black (3) octagons under the purple stripes serve to underline the antique theme.

saturated/**Grape Basket**

In this style of quilt, in which a clearly defined object is set into a background, obviously the choice of background is a determining factor in the final effect. In **Gold Standard** the background contrasts well with the pieced basket, but is quite dark in tone, so imparts a dignified and regal atmosphere to the quilt. The sky blue background in **Serene Skies**, on the other hand, means that the general effect is calm and peaceful.

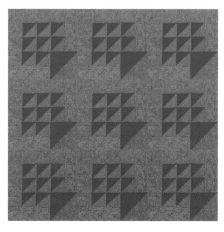

1
2
3
Gem Stone Quilt The combination of deep amethyst (3) and turquoise (2) sheds a jewel-like brilliance, enhanced by juxtaposing the turquoise to the dark patterned (1) background to gain maximum impact from the contrast.

Grape Basket template
This template shows the individual pieces of a block, irrespective of color.

1
2
3
Flying Geese Emphasis is on the intense blue (3) triangles pieced in the form of a traditional "flying geese" pattern, which contrast well with the golden brown (2). Contrast between the brown triangles and the background (1) is muted, so the blue stands out even more clearly.

1
2
3
Imperial Touch Red and purple always look regal together. Intense strawberry red (3) in the basket and purple (1) in the background are separated by a soft, warm coffee brown (2), which contrasts well with the purple without detracting from the generally opulent look of the quilt.

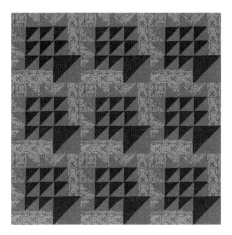

❶❷❸ Gold Standard The main contrast is between the gold (1) of the background and complementary royal blue (2) triangles. The deep reddish brown (3) triangles, although mostly separated from it, works with the gold background to unify the scheme.

❶❷❸ Serene Skies Emerald green (2) next to complementary rust (3) gives the pieced basket strong definition but, when placed on the sky blue background (1), the overall effect is calm and tranquil.

❶❷❸ Fire Baskets Hot, intense carmine red (2) and the even more intense orange (3) make a fiery combination, which glows against the dark brown (1) background in a very dramatic color scheme.

❶❷❸ Basket of Lemons Bright green (2) and lemon yellow (3), despite being on the same side of the color wheel, make a dazzling combination when a lighter tone of yellow is used. There is less contrast between the green and the dusky pink (1) background, so the yellow stands out all the more brightly.

SEVEN-PATCH BLOCKS

saturated/**Bear's Paw**

Bear's Paw can look cool and classic, as in **Paw Prints**, or dark and dramatic, like **Emerald Trellis**. When the paler colors are used for the long center patches and surrounding triangles, the "paw" effect is emphasized, seen particularly clearly in **Paw Prints**. In **Touch of Turquoise**, when a dark tone is used for the patches, the eye focuses more on the overall design of rectangles, squares, and triangles.

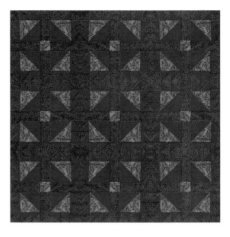

❶ ❷ ❸ Touch of Turquoise A small proportion of turquoise (3) injects a touch of brilliance into a very warm, rich combination of terra cotta (1) and intense, glowing gold (2), creating a series of focal points without detracting from the general impression of opulence.

Bear's Paw template
This template shows the individual pieces of a block, irrespective of color.

❶ ❷ ❸ Intensely Pink The pinkish (1) background contains a touch of blue, so the contrast with the blue (2) itself is muted, but the outlines of the "paws" motif are still clear. The green (3) is an unobtrusive contrast to the blue but, being complementary to the pink, gives the scheme unity.

❶ ❷ ❸ Paw Prints A clear contrast between the pale yellow (1) background, seen as a neutral, and the intense brownish pink (2) and green (3) gives strong emphasis to the "paw" shapes. The contrast between warm pink and pale lemon is slightly moderated by the introduction of the touch of green.

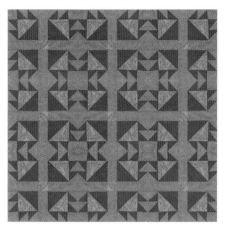

①②③ Emerald Trellis Intense tones of reddish pink (2) and green (1) receive added dramatic impact from the introduction of a judicious proportion of black (3). The subsidiary patterns seen in the repeated blocks are emphasized by the green shapes rather than being dominated by them.

①②③ Cool and Classic A neutral, very pale apple green (2) is a foil for the darker tone of green (1), complemented by a softer grape purple (3), the final effect being surprisingly cool and traditional in feel.

①②③ Softly, Softly A very warm, soothing color scheme, in which the deep brownish pink (2) sinks into a paler, dusky pink (1) background, with pale donkey brown (3) giving just enough contrast without impinging too much on the rest of the pattern.

①②③ Inner Glow Similar tones of all three colors give each of the elements of the pattern the same importance, but there is sufficient resonance between the blue (2) and complementary gold (1) to reveal the shapes. The deep purplish pink (3) imparts an inner glow to the "paw" motifs.

saturated/**Lincoln's Platform**

A simple, easily read pattern like Lincoln's Platform gains all its effect from the mood evoked by the juxtaposition of colors. Pink, blue, and yellow in **Summer Days**, for example, elicit a cheerful, optimistic mood, while **Mountain View**, where the saturated brown is set against softer colors, reflects a calm, serene mood. Black and yellow are considered one of the most visible color combinations to use, so **Black and Gold** is bound to make a strong graphic impact.

1 2 3 Black and Gold Vivid marigold (1) and blue (2), a vibrant combination in itself, gets even stronger impact when the blocks are outlined in black (3). The juxtaposition of the black and yellow maximizes this effect.

1 2 3 Little Buttercup Chestnut brown (1) and buttercup yellow (2) lie under strips of jade green (3), which, being used proportionately less than the other colors, adds a lively touch to the more earthy hues without overwhelming them.

Lincoln's Platform template This template shows the individual pieces of a block, irrespective of color.

1 2 3 Exotic Touch Slightly subdued tones of plush reddish plum (1) combined with deep blue (2) look rich and dense. The lighter, brighter tomato red (3), contributes a touch of brilliance resulting in a sophisticated color scheme with a distinctly exotic feel to it.

①②③ Orange Dots Deep purplish blue (1) and an intense complementary orange (2) make a vibrant combination, but the overall effect is softened by the introduction of a neutral, very light beige (3). This makes the major visual impact, while at the same time highlighting the orange in the center of each block.

①②③ Mountain View A greater proportion of slate gray (1) casts a generally soft atmosphere over the intense peat brown (2) and heather purple (3), so the atmosphere is calm and reflective, evoking distance and natural landscapes.

①②③ On the Bright Side Brilliant pink (1) and complementary green (2) always make a vibrant impact, but the addition of charcoal gray (3) tones the whole scheme down and gives it a softer, more sophisticated feel.

①②③ Summer Days Intense tones of blue (1) and pink (2) are bright and summery, the lighthearted mood being enhanced by the addition of sunshine yellow (3). A cheerful, optimistic color scheme, this could make a pleasing quilt for a child's room.

saturated/**Claws**

Saturated colors can be effectively combined with lighter, more subdued colors to achieve varying effects. In **Orange Fizz** all the colors are deep and intense and the final effect depends on the contrast between the two complementary colors, whereas in **Pink Stars** the introduction of a much paler tone of the darker, more intense colors results in a harmonious color scheme in which the stars are the main focus.

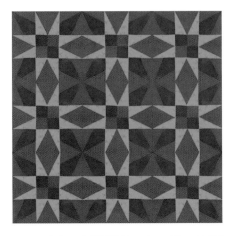

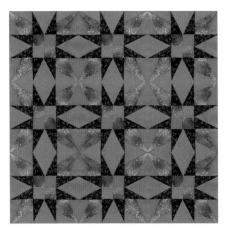

①
②
❸ **Orange Fizz** Although intense gentian blue (1) certainly holds its own in this dazzling color scheme, it's the deep orange (2) that dominates, emphasizing the diagonal shapes of crosses and squares. The deep blue (3) stars act as backup in a strong, vibrant scheme.

Claws template
This template shows the individual pieces of a block, irrespective of color.

①
②
❸ **Emerald Sky** Plum purple (1) and purplish blue (2) tend to recede slightly behind the more vibrant emerald green (3) stars, an effect enhanced by the hint of pink in both the background colors, which reduces the contrast between them.

①
②
❸ **Red Stars Quilt** Plenty of contrast between the deep blue (1) and olive green (2) make them a lively background to the lighter tones of the strawberry red (3). The red stars, though, are still the main players in a strong, assertive color scheme.

 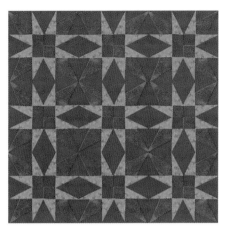

 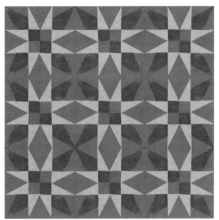

(1) (2) (3) Green Shadows Three colors of similar tone give each element of the pattern equal value, but the two greens (1, 2) tend to merge to form a shadowy background to the blue (3) so that the stars emerge unobtrusively. A quilt in which deep tones combine in a dignified, understated scheme.

(1) (2) (3) Hint of Fall Glowing tones of warm, autumnal browns (1, 3) highlight the cooler, deep turquoise (2) corner points in each block, so the eye focuses on the diagonal lines of the pattern.

(1) (2) (3) Complementary Stars Intense tones of complementary puce pink (2) and emerald green (3) together make a splash, but because the charcoal gray (1) has a subtle pink tinge to it, the impact between that and the pink is reduced when the two colors meet. The green therefore takes center stage.

(1) (2) (3) Pink Stars Two tones of deep, mauvish purple (1, 2) are set with much paler mauve (3) star points, which appear to join and emphasize the vertical and horizontal directions of the design in a pleasingly harmonious color scheme.

saturated/**Puss in the Corner**

Although it is the fabric chosen for the long patches, sometimes appearing to join and form squares, that tends to be the decisive factor in the design, much variation can still be achieved by careful juxtaposition of colors and tones. In **Restraining Influence** the squares are seen under a network of discreetly contrasting gray, and this same effect can be seen in **Mandarin Squares**. In **Bold and Distinctive** and **Echoing Tones**, the illusion of diagonally set squares is complete.

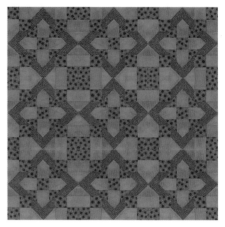

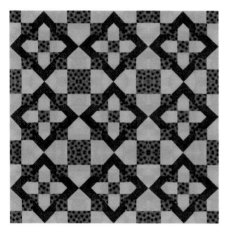

①
②
③ **Bold and Distinctive** An unusual combination of deep blue (1) and lime green (2) has impact because of the distinctly yellow tinge in the green. Use of black (3) for the outlining square shapes emphasizes still more the bold and distinctive character of this color scheme.

Puss in the Corner template This template shows the individual pieces of a block, irrespective of color.

①
②
③ **Restraining Influence** The strong impact of intense tones of brilliant complementary green (2) and fuchsia (3) is seen under the restraining influence of a network of mottled gray (1) squares, which seem to join up and lie on top of the green and pink shapes.

①
②
③ **Intense Harmony** Dark mustard yellow (1) and brown (3) are offset against a background of neutral cream (2), the contrast between light and dark highlighting the pattern of crosses inside squares. The particular tone of the cream, which echoes the mustard yellow, creates a quiet and harmonious final effect.

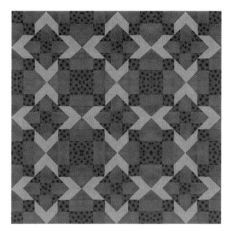

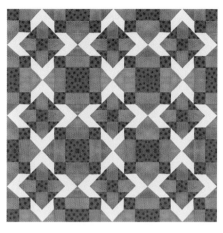

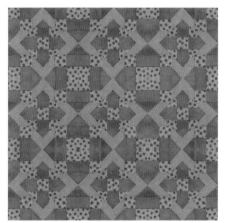

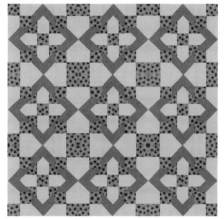

1 2 3 **Green Highlights** The slightly exotic atmosphere created by the combination of intense tones of deep, purplish blue (1) and magenta (2) is intensified rather than subdued by the addition of a brilliant green (3), the tension between warm and cool colors adding a little frisson to the scheme.

1 2 3 **Mandarin Squares** Because of the slightly brighter tone of the mandarin orange (3), there is a visual illusion of complete squares lying under the pattern formed by the turquoise (1) and gray (2) shapes. Contrast between the orange and complementary turquoise also creates a strong color scheme.

1 2 3 **Echoing Tones** Set against deep tones of purple (1) and mustard yellow (2), squares formed by the very pale yellow (3) emerge as the dominant theme of the design. However, the whole quilt is unified by the echoing tones, pale and dark, of yellow.

1 2 3 **Balancing Act** A pleasing, well-balanced design achieved by using colors of similar tones but with contrast provided by magenta (3) patches, which are on the opposite side of the color wheel to the green (1) and yellow (2). The juxtaposition of magenta and green clearly defines the pattern of crosses.

saturated/**Star of the East**

This quickly and easily pieced pattern offers infinite possibilities for variation in style and mood, from the cheerful, optimistic **Bright and Breezy** to the darker and more dramatic atmosphere of **Starry Drama**. A pronounced three-dimensional effect appears when light and dark tones of the same color are chosen for the two sides of the star blades, although this effect can be modified: the gray background of **Subtle Stars** softens it, while the strongly contrasting background of **Eastern Gold** emphasizes it.

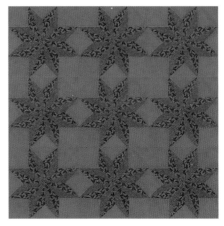

1 2 3 Added Spice Intense, spicy gold (1) makes a rich and glowing background to the more somber blue (2) and dark chocolate brown (3) of the stars, adding an extra dimension to a color scheme for an otherwise practical, user-friendly quilt.

1 2 3 Subtle Stars The gentle, mouse gray (1) background has a generally softening effect on the stronger, more vibrant violet (2) and pink (3) of the stars. The faceted effect of the stars becomes very subtle, in keeping with the generally restful and soothing overall effect.

Star of the East template This template shows the individual pieces of a block, irrespective of color.

1 2 3 Bright and Breezy In this combination the deep sea green (1) is in stronger contrast to the bright orange (2) than to the purplish blue (3), giving dominance to the orange. However, strong contrast between the two colors used in the star ensure that they still have plenty of impact.

1 2 3 **Woodland Theme** The deep-dyed tone of grass green (1) makes a sympathetic background for stars with slightly earthy colors, nut brown (2) and yellowish tan (3), in a quilt with a mellow atmosphere evoking woodland colors.

1 2 3 **Eastern Gold** Three-dimensional effect stars, achieved by juxtaposition of medium aqua (2) and deep blue (3), are given maximum impact when set against a background of deep-dyed complementary gold (1). A classic combination of colors, typical of Moorish decorative design.

1 2 3 **Starry Drama** Complementary aqua (2) and bright orange (3) make a dramatic statement when set on a black (1) background in an unequivocally strong and assertive color scheme. The use of black for the background emphasizes the linear construction of the design.

1 2 3 **Burnt Orange** The combination of dark chocolate (2) and the brighter tone of the burnt orange (3) could be a little hard on the eye, but the green (1) background imparts a slightly restful atmosphere without detracting from the generally positive and cheerful mood of the quilt.

saturated/**Virginia Star**

With Virginia Star, background color often determines the final mood of the quilt, especially when using deep tones, which need careful placement. In **Fruits and Cream**, placing rich colors on a neutral background lightens the whole mood. Black, as in **Dark Windows**, always throws the other colors into relief, but it's wise to use a slightly brighter color immediately next to it to sharpen the definition of the pattern.

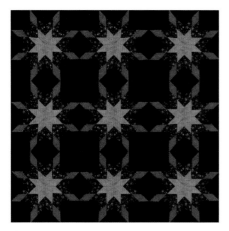

❶❷❸❹ Dark Windows Black (1) squares and diamonds appear below the starry grid formed by scarlet (2) points on the stars, which seem to join up and emphasize the pattern's grid structure. Complementary purple (3) against olive green (4) gives a necessary, lighter focal point in an otherwise dramatic color scheme.

1 2 3 4 Fruits and Cream A combination of fruity colors, deep-dyed damson blue (2) and magenta (3), with a splash of olive green (4) in the center, acquire a bright, lighthearted atmosphere when placed on a neutral background of pale cream (1).

Virginia Star template
This template shows the individual pieces of a block, irrespective of color.

❶❷❸❹ Blue Eyes The olive (1) background, the brownish purple (2) points of the stars, and the ring of terra-cotta (3) diamonds create quite a subdued effect, so the brilliant blue (4) stars at the center of the blocks become the focal point, and create a lively and interesting scheme.

1 2 3 4 **Winning Combination** The attention-grabbing combination of charcoal gray (1) and vibrant orange (2) focuses the eye on the large squares and diamonds, while the green (3) stars, with their magenta (4) centers appear to sit on the junctions of the grid.

1 2 3 4 **Pretty Peach** Pretty peach (1) forms a soothing background to the more intense and assertive colors. Deep fuchsia pink (2) set around complementary aqua (3) gives the stars definition and the scheme is unified by the use of nut brown (4) in the center, toning subtly with the background peach.

1 2 3 4 **Summer Suns** Burnt orange (1) imparts a warm, fiery glow to this quilt, an effect intensified by the bright gold (4) of the star centers. The centers are given added impact by the ring of mottled purple (3) diamonds around them and the green (2) points of the stars, contrasting well with the background.

1 2 3 4 **Elegant Blue** Limited contrast between the two plum colors (3, 4) in the center blurs the shapes to create a gentle, muted effect, the dark blue (2) points giving just enough definition against the sky blue (1) background. The overall effect is quite serene and elegant.

saturated/**Bow Tie**

Schemes based on saturated colors naturally tend to be rich and glowing, for example **Opulence**, but lighter effects can be achieved by adding brighter colors in greater or lesser proportions. **Olive Oil** positively radiates light when bright olive green is used for large octagons, and **Garnet Stones** gets a lift from the brighter tone of red. All the quilts shown here illustrate the infinite versatility of a block based on very simple geometric shapes when colors and tones are carefully manipulated.

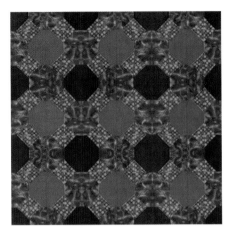

Opulence Maroon (2) and mottled purple (3) prints contribute texture and complexity to the design, in which deep purple (1) tends to recede, with the octagons in intense, deep-dyed orange (4) shining out to enhance the opulent overall effect.

Emerald Glow Black (1) octagons alternating with those in mottled purple (3) and shocking pink (4) give maximum definition to all the shapes. The emerald green (2) squares also catch the eye, and appear as a network across the surface.

Bow Tie template
This template shows the individual pieces of a block, irrespective of color.

Lancaster County A combination of navy (1), electric blue (2), and jade (3) makes a cool background to the fiery red (4) octagons in a vibrant color scheme that is characteristic of the Amish quilts of Lancaster County.

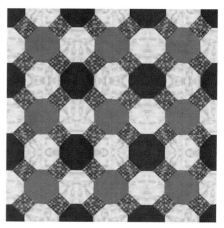

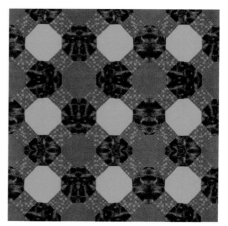

Garnet Stones The garnet (2) squares are brighter in tone than the other colors, so the pattern they make tends to dominate the design. However, aqua (3) and azure blue (4) are also strong elements of the design, while dark purple (1) tends to recede into a supporting role.

Deep Pools Deep bluish purple (1) octagons look a little subdued when alternating with emerald green (2) squares and bright pink (3) octagons, which can be interpreted as a pattern surrounding the pools of prominent black (4) octagons.

Olive Oil The glow of olive oil is captured in this quilt where dark olive green (2) squares surround octagons in a much more vibrant tone of olive (3) and deep plum (4). Dark indigo (1) adds depth without detracting from the glowing overall effect.

Ebony Brooches A strong contrast between the mottled black (3) and its surrounding colors ensures that it plays the central role. Deep puce (1) and green (4) in similar tones and slightly purple (2) squares emphasize the diagonal elements of the design and reinforce the pattern of black octagons.

saturated/**Kaleidoscope**

Saturated colors can be used effectively with other tones for a variety of effects. The addition of very dark tones or black, for example, always makes for a winning combination, because it gives maximum intensity to the other colors, as you can see in **Swirling Colors**. In **Indigo Shadows**, a bright color is used to add necessary focal points to a deep, rich color scheme that could otherwise appear too somber.

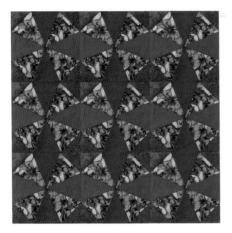

 Swirling Colors Deep tones of pink (1) and an even deeper tone of complementary turquoise (3) have been "lifted" from the vivid, multicolored print (2), combining with it to create a vibrant quilt in which shapes and colors seem to swirl rhythmically over the surface.

Mellow Yellow Old gold (2) and olive green (3) make a pleasingly mellow combination, the slightly brighter yellow emphasizing the triangle patches and making them a good foil for the green diamonds. Purple (1) corners show up well against complementary yellow and add a little touch of opulence.

Royal Flush Brick red (3) diamonds appear to lie over deep purple (2) octagons in a color combination that carries a suggestion of regal pomp, while the golden olive (1) squares between the main shapes underscore this effect.

Kaleidoscope template
This template shows the individual pieces of a block, irrespective of color.

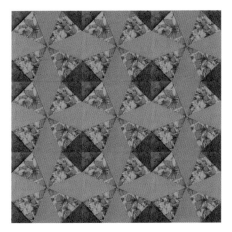

1 2 3 **Bright Octagons** Octagons in bright kingfisher blue (2), contrasting strongly with the mustard (1) squares, light up the surface of the quilt, and together form a background to the pattern of greenish yellow (3) diamonds.

1 2 3 **Amish Influence** When black (1) squares are used between shapes formed by bright eggshell blue (2) and a deeper tone of mulberry (3), the main shapes of diamonds and triangles make maximum visual impact in a classic color combination.

1 **Indigo Shadows** Similar tones of deep jade green (3) and indigo (2) tend to merge to form a shadowy pattern, separated by a series of focal points provided by brighter gold (1) squares, adding the necessary light touch while at the same time pointing up the generally shadowy effect.

1 2 3 **Pink Wheels** Rosy pink (2) triangles come forward a little from the more intense tones of emerald green (1) and plum (3), and looked at in one way can be seen to join and form interlocking circles across the surface.

saturated/**Lattice and Square**

Combine saturated colors with those in either brighter or more sober tones—carefully selected to enhance the deeper colors—to create desired moods and effects, and highlight different elements of the pattern. The squares-on-point made by the long rectangle patches usually dominate the scene, in **Jet Squares** because they are inky black and in **Wake-up Quilt** because they are significantly brighter. However, other elements of the pattern can be highlighted, as in **Well-balanced**, where the blue squares come into focus.

1 **2** **3** **Jet Squares** Characteristically Amish colors create their brilliant, jewel-like effect in this quilt, the jet black (3) squares making maximum impact against glowing emerald green (2) and deep purple (1).

1 **2** **3** **Wake-up Quilt** Warm, cheerful brick red (1) and dark tan (2) get a lift from sunshine yellow (3), which, being brighter in tone, gives the diagonally set squares pride of place, while the tan squares recede and merge into the red. The perfect quilt to wake up to in the morning.

1 **2** **3** **Light Touch** Deep, saturated blue (1) is juxtaposed to a slightly brighter tone of olive (2), against which the nut-brown (3) squares tend to recede, so that the olive appears even brighter and gives an otherwise sober and dignified quilt the necessary lighter touch.

Lattice and Square template This template shows the individual pieces of a block, irrespective of color.

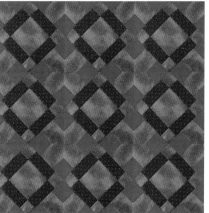

1 **2** **3** **Well-balanced** Long patches in greenish yellow (3) stand out as squares-on-point, alternating with orange (1) squares with indigo blue (2) corners. The juxtaposition of complementary blue and orange in intense tones means those shapes emerge strongly, resulting in a pleasing, well-balanced design.

1 **2** **3** **High Victorian Style** Contrast between the green (1) and purple (2) is slightly subdued, so the shapes they form appear as a background to the dark charcoal gray (3) that sets the mood for a rather sultry scheme. The green and purple lend a subtle glow to the quilt.

1 **2** **3** **Quiet Appeal** Contrast between cool green (1) and warm pink (3) gives the quilt a gentle radiance, with deep purple (2) squares acting as backup in a quilt with quiet, understated appeal.

1 **2** **3** **Twist of Lime** Deep-dyed purple (1) and squares of black (2) set off the intense lime green (3) of the squares formed by the long patches, which stand out as the main focus across the surface and turn what might otherwise be a slightly somber combination into a more vibrant design.

saturated/**Washington Pavement**

The strongly patterned print in the corners and centers of the blocks ensures a high degree of visual texture, whatever the color combination may be, and it enhances and intensifies the surrounding deep-dyed and saturated colors, guaranteeing satisfyingly complex surfaces every time. This is most apparent in **Rich and Complex**, a dazzling combination of reds and blues, but even where colors are less vibrant, such as in **Lime Grove** and **Purple Squares**, the effects are still striking.

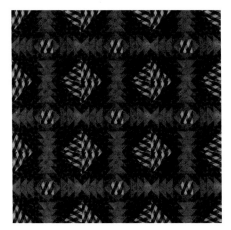

❶ ❷ ❸ Rich and Complex Intense colors in a strongly patterned fabric (1) set the tone for a wonderfully rich, complex design in which midnight blue (2) squares are surrounded by a network of deep pink (3) serrated lines.

❶ ❷ ❸ Deep Fuchsia Shapes in deep fuchsia (2) are the main elements of the pattern, given added definition when separated by mottled gray (1) squares. Pine green (3) triangles lie lightly on top to brighten the overall effect.

Washington Pavement template This template shows the individual pieces of a block, irrespective of color.

❶ ❷ ❸ Dynamic Surface A grid of bright acid lemon (3) triangles turns this combination of intense green patterned with black (1) and purple (2) into an excitingly dynamic quilt surface.

Striking Combination Deep tones of blue (2) juxtaposed to complementary orange (3) can't fail to make a striking combination, the effect here enhanced by the introduction of an olive green and black print (1). The lines of orange triangles seem to lie over the blue background.

Subtle Restraint Reddish orange (2) octagons emerge and are given maximum definition when separated by the electric blue (1) squares, with gray (3) triangles apparently lying over them and exercising subtle restraint on the whole scheme.

Lime Grove The shocking pink (1) is used in small proportions to highlight shapes in deep-dyed indigo blue (2), with lime green (3) in a lighter, brighter tone making a network over the entire surface and imparting a very lively overall atmosphere.

Purple Squares Purple (2) squares behind golden tan (1) squares-on-point are the main focus of the pattern, which is overlaid by a grid of leaf green (3) triangles that contrast well with the purple but are not so bright as to dominate the design.

saturated/**Winding Ways**

The swirling circle and petal shapes of Winding Ways can be very effective when pieced in intense, saturated colors. Strong contrast between the two colors tends to produce sharper, more clearly defined shapes, as you can see in **Subtle Drama** and **Looks Exotic**. Keeping the tones similar, as in **Warm Glow** and **Competition Time**, tends to add complexity, because the eye constantly seeks to interpret the pattern in different ways.

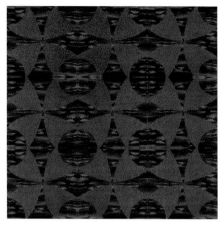

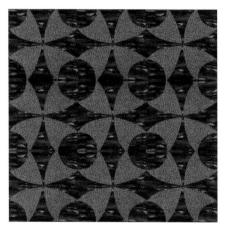

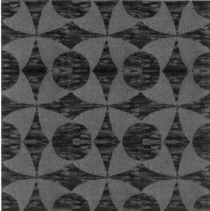

1
2 **Warm Glow** A warm and glowing quilt in which the circles and diamonds in burgundy (1) appear between swirling shapes of old gold (2). The gold is just bright enough to come forward so that the burgundy shapes lie in the background.

1
2 **Subtle Drama** When black (1) is juxtaposed to deep puce (2) the effect is always going to be dramatic, but here that effect is subtly modified by the fact that the black is mottled with gray, rather than being jet black.

Winding Ways template
This template shows the individual pieces of a block, irrespective of color.

1
2 **Discreet Resonance** Deep olive (2), containing a hint of luster, set on a background of mottled plum (1) makes a rich combination. The fact that the two colors are on opposite sides of the color wheel adds a discreet resonance to the scheme.

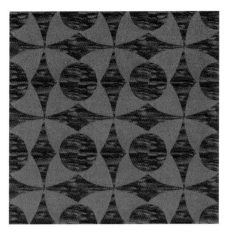

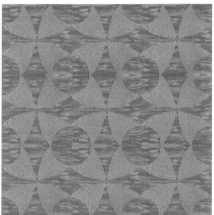

❶
❷ **Deep Blush** Two rich, warm reds, one burgundy (1) and the other cyclamen (2), in an appreciably brighter tone, give maximum emphasis to both the large curves made by the cyclamen patches and the darker shapes between them.

❶
❷ **Looks Exotic** A combination of midnight blue (1) and shocking pink (2) has a distinctly exotic look about it, the contrast between the two colors giving all the shapes clear definition.

❶
❷ **Competition Time** The shapes in orange (1) and gold (2), both in intense tones, compete for attention so that all the elements of the pattern are outlined and defined, creating visual complexity as the eye seeks to interpret the pattern in different ways.

❶
❷ **Gray Petals** Gray (2) petal shapes recede behind olive (1) circles and diamonds in a very subtle, understated color scheme, ideal for a quilt to be part of a cool, elegant décor.

saturated/**Round Table**

Round Table pieced in intense, saturated colors is the perfect way to make a big impression with a single block. A cheerful, bouncing mood is evoked in **Black Buttons** and **Cooling Touch** by strong contrast in the main shapes, while more muted contrast between the main colors in **Full Moons** gives a deeper, mysterious atmosphere. The center circle puts the finishing touch to the scheme, lighting it up, as in **Full Moons** and **Hint of Spring**, or exerting a restraining influence, as in **Black Buttons** and **Cooling Touch**.

1 **2** **3** **Spiced Up** Deep blue (1) and rich lime green (2) are gently vibrant together, but the introduction of deep spicy orange (3), which is complementary to the blue, completely changes the atmosphere and lifts the mood.

1 **2** **3** **Black Buttons** Bouncing balls of tangerine (1) and complementary electric blue (2) could be a touch garish, but the series of black (3) "buttons" adds competing focal points without detracting from the generally dynamic impression of the quilt.

1 **2** **3** **Full Moons** Glowing emerald green (1) and black (2) combine in a rich, jewel-bright pattern that looks dense and slightly mysterious, so that the yellow (3) circles lying on top of the surface shine out like a series of full moons.

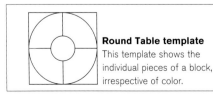

Round Table template
This template shows the individual pieces of a block, irrespective of color.

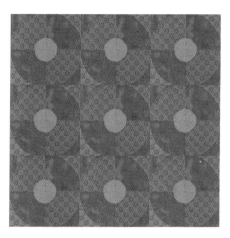

1 **Quiet Mood** Tan (1) and complementary
2 turquoise (2) contrast well together, but a
3 quiet mood is imparted by the addition of the
yellowish olive (3) in a slightly subdued tone.

1 **Cooling Touch** Indigo blue (1) and
2 complementary orange (2) combine to create
3 a positively radiant quilt surface. The very pale
green (3) circles, contrasting well with both
colors, add a cooling touch to make a striking
color scheme just a little easier on the eye.

1 **Hint of Spring** Natural, earthy colors of
2 deep-dyed tan (1) and vibrant grassy green
3 (2) are well matched in a color scheme
holding a hint of spring, the impression
being underscored by the addition of pale
primrose (3) circles.

1 **Spotlights** Olive green (1) and purple (2) are
2 always a pleasing combination, and a series of
3 pale, neutral cream (3) spotlights points up
the contrast between the two main colors and
lights up the surface.

saturated/**Japanese Fan**

Discreetly Bright and **Green Field Fans** illustrate the way in which marked contrast between the two colors used in the fans emphasizes their checkered effect and makes them stand out from the background, whereas in **Flash of Pink** and **Orange Rims** the fans are more muted and would tend to sink into the background without their brighter arcs and strips. When Japanese Fans are pieced in rich saturated tones they capture a little of the color and magic of the Far East, as you can see in **Dark and Mysterious**.

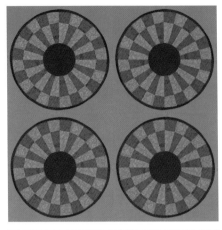

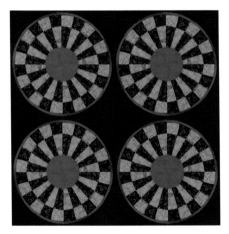

1 **2** **3** **4** **Dark and Mysterious** Black (1) imparts mystery and richness to any color scheme with intense colors. Here, there is a rich glowing quality to the combination of gold (2) and purple (3) in the fans, enhanced by the insertion of emerald green (4) between black and the other colors.

1 **2** **3** **4** **Touch of Black** A background of glowing emerald green (1) is a perfect foil for deep violet (2) and pink (3) in the fans. The touch of black (4), in arcs and rims, clearly defines the contrast between the fans and their background, and makes the deep-dyed colors look even more intense.

1 **2** **3** **4** **Discreetly Bright** There is a discreet brightness in these fans, pieced in yellow (2) and grassy green (3), then outlined in pale neutral cream (4). They stand out clearly from the indigo (1) background, chosen to add a little vibrancy.

Japanese Fan template
This template shows the individual pieces of a block, irrespective of color.

①②③④ Flash of Pink A rich, dense combination of deep tones of purple (2) and turquoise (3) is set on an equally dark background of petrol blue (1), so that the contrasting center circles and outer rims of candy pink (4) come out as flashes of brightness, adding a touch of drama.

①②③④ Orange Rims Muted contrast between the dark olive (2) and brown (3) used in the fans gives them a subdued impact, but they gain strong definition when outlined by bright orange (4) circles and rims, juxtaposed to a background in complementary navy blue (1).

①②③④ Black-and-blue Black (2) and electric blue (3) in the fans make a striking combination, very slightly subdued by the addition of dusky purple (4) circles and rims. When the fans are set on a mustard yellow (1) background the overall effect is calm and restrained.

①②③④ Green Field Fans Deepest plum (2) is juxtaposed to bright marigold (3), the strong contrast between these complementary colors emphasizing the checkered effect. When set on a bright green (1) background the result is a rich, opulent scheme, with gray (4) circles and rims imparting a slightly sobering effect.

saturated/**Friendship Fan**

Whether warm and glowing, like **Intensely Pink** and **Bush Fire**, or crisply defined, like **Golden Afternoon**, all the Friendship Fans pieced in saturated colors make strong graphic statements. In **Dazzling Impression** the inclusion of a touch of black gives even more intensity to the other colors. Striking a softer note, **Sotto Voce** uses slightly muted tones of pink and green, and the sultry effect is enhanced by the addition of a small proportion of gray.

1 **2** **3** **Intensely Pink** Cool/warm contrast between vivid cerise (1) and medium aqua (2) gives this quilt a dynamic vibrancy, and the intensity of the colors gives a sense of luxury that is enhanced and exaggerated by a series of indigo (3) circles across the surface.

1 **2** **3** **Dazzling Impression** Deep violet (1) and hot red (2) together make a dazzling impression, but it is the red, in a slightly brighter tone, that is the most eye-catching feature of the scheme. Black (3) rings serve to make the other colors look even more intense and glowing.

1 **2** **3** **Dynamic Combination** Cyclamen pink (1) and electric blue (2) make a striking and dynamic combination, and could even look a little garish, so deep olive circles (3), because they have subdued contrast with the pink, add a note of restraint.

Friendship Fan template This template shows the individual pieces of a block, irrespective of color.

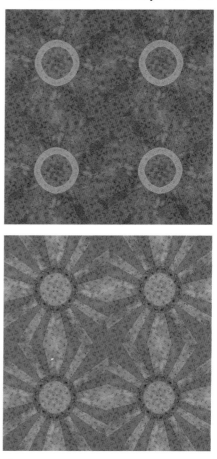

1 **Bush Fire** Two fiery colors, orange (1) and
2 tomato red (2), evoke images of fiercely
3 burning flames, with bright yellow (3) circles
flickering across the surface. The "fire" theme
is echoed in the shape of the fan blades.

1 **Sotto Voce** Complementary pink (1) and
2 green (2) are used in very subtly muted tones,
3 and when soft gray (3) circles are added the
overall effect is surprisingly rich and soft—and
even just a little sultry.

1 **Light Relief** Purple (1) and golden tan (2)
2 look rich and dense together, so the circles
3 in pale, neutral cream (3) stand out as focal
points across the surface and add a little
light relief.

1 **Golden Afternoon** Combining a mellow
2 tone of glowing gold (1) with brilliant sky blue
3 (2) can't fail to produce a stunning quilt that
evokes the mood of a hot summer's day, with
emerald green (3) circles adding just a
suggestion of coolness.

saturated/**Bleeding Hearts**

This block provides plenty of scope for matching and contrasting intense colors and, as you can see, the effects can be startlingly varied. Combined with black or even very dark colors, saturated colors are always striking and dramatic, as seen in **Spitfire**, **Jade Lights**, and **High Visibility**. On the other hand, when matched with cooler, paler colors, as in **Muted Elegance**, a calmer, more sedate atmosphere is conveyed.

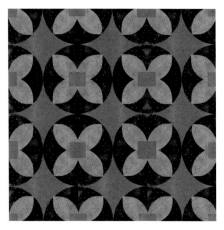

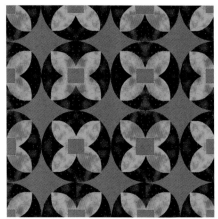

1 2 3 Spitfire Brilliant contrast between curve-sided squares in fiery orange (1), alternating with midnight blue (3) circles, makes for a vivid combination, only slightly moderated by placing pale aqua (2) petal shapes on the circles.

1 2 3 Vivid impression Pairing vivid yellow (1) with complementary deep-dyed violet (3) serves to emphasize both the brilliant colors and the contrast between them. Brighter, greenish-blue (2) petals give the circles even greater importance in a bright and lively design with lots of movement.

1 2 3 Jade Lights A softer, but no less pleasing, version of the Spitfire quilt, here deep cyclamen pink (1) is juxtaposed to black (3) circles topped by jade green (2) petals to lighten and brighten, while at the same time exaggerating the dramatic overall effect of intense colors juxtaposed to black.

Bleeding Hearts template This template shows the individual pieces of a block, irrespective of color.

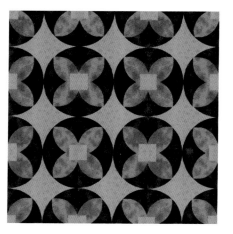

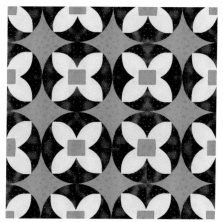

1 **2** **3** **Hint of Luxury** The combination of deep olive (1) and indigo (3) has a hint of luxury about it, a quality enhanced by the addition of warm, soft red (2), which resonates gently with the olive so that overall the quilt has a touch of oriental exoticism about it.

1 **2** **3** **Muted Elegance** Pale beige (1) exerts a softening influence on the whole surface so that although the intense colors, cyclamen pink (2) and deep-dyed indigo (3), make a strong statement, the scheme has a quiet, well-balanced elegance.

1 **2** **3** **Clear Definition** Bright greenish yellow (1) and green (3) contrast well together, giving all the shapes equal emphasis. Placing almost complementary bright pink (2) petals over the green circles adds yet another dimension to a strong and vibrant design.

1 **2** **3** **High Visibility** Placing black with vivid colors makes them look even brighter and more dramatic, and by juxtaposing yellow (2) to black (3), always a highly visible combination, the effect is even more pronounced, with the deep blue (1) taking on a jewel-like quality.

APPLIQUÉ BLOCKS

saturated/**Dutch Tulips**

A high degree of visual ambiguity is revealed in Dutch Tulips when intense colors are played against either very dark or very light backgrounds. In **Midnight Bloom** and **Vibrant Yellow** the main shapes made by the tulip heads make the first and most obvious impression, largely because they are set on much darker backgrounds. When light backgrounds are used, the shapes that they form in the repeated blocks gain greater significance in the overall design.

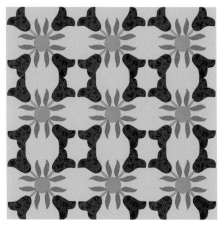

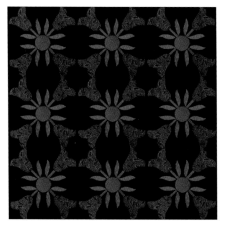

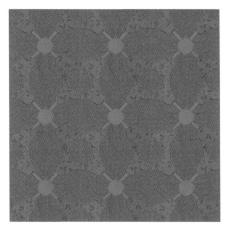

1 2 3 4 **Midnight Bloom** Deep-dyed colors gain even more intensity when set on a black (1) background. The use of deep fuchsia pink (2) with complementary green (3), plus a touch of electric blue (4), guarantees that this quilt has maximum visual impact.

1 2 3 4 **Background Lights** A neutral (1) background produces distinctive shapes in repeated blocks that become the setting for dark reddish brown (2) tulips, alternating with florets of deep blue (3) and pink (4) in intense tones. The final effect is a strong, crisp design.

1 2 3 4 **Calm Center** Similar tones for the olive green (1) background and violet (3) leaves cause them to recede a little, compared with the very slightly brighter pink (2). All the shapes appear to join and form circles across the surface, with blue-gray (4) stems and center circles injecting a slightly calming note.

Dutch Tulips template
This template shows the individual pieces of a block, irrespective of color.

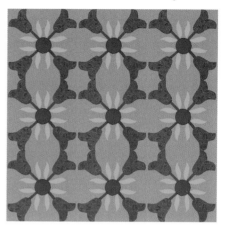

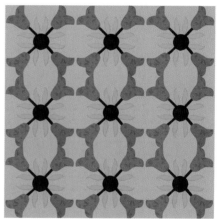

①②③④ Vibrant Yellow Vibrant yellow (2) against a dark brown (1) background is guaranteed to achieve visual impact. Florets of kingfisher blue (4) stems and circles, surrounded by green leaves (3), stand out well against the background, alternating with the yellow shapes to make a strong, well-balanced scheme.

①②③④ Lilac Highlights The dark bluish green (1) background is in a similar tone to the deep pinkish red (2) flowers and blue (3) leaves, leaving the lilac (4) stems and centers, pieced in a slightly brighter tone, to catch the eye and emphasize the diagonal elements, the overall effect being rather rich and dense.

①②③④ Color and Complexity An intense tone of burnt orange (2) makes the first impact, but the shapes made by the brighter pearl gray (1) background also appear, and can be read either as circles containing the orange shapes, or as lantern shapes with florets of green (3) leaves and purple (4) stems at their centers.

①②③④ Center Accent In an intriguingly ambiguous design, the pale gray (1) shapes are a background to florets of jade (3) and dark brown (4), which become the main focus and are seen between curve-sided squares in dusky violet (2) formed by the tulip heads. A striking and sophisticated color scheme.

Tints

When white is added
to a color, the resulting light
values of it are tints. Use tints to
capture carefree, youthful moods and
also as contrast to more assertive color
combinations. Tints can have varying degrees of
brightness, depending on the basic color and the
proportion of white in them. Color schemes based on tints
are usually pretty and feminine, and are ideal choices for
occasions when you aim for a light-hearted, summery effect.
In quilts based entirely on tints, choose colors which have
sufficient contrast or, if using similar colors, choose
those with varying degrees of brightness.
Tints can also be used as neutrals and work
beautifully as backgrounds to darker
and more distinct colors.

tints/**Cross and Square**

Subtle and interesting pattern variations are seen when tints are applied to Cross and Square. In **Poplars**, contrast between pale lime green and blue causes the stars to appear clear and crisp, while in **Blossom Time** they almost vanish because of the subdued contrast between the pink and green. In **Tartan Weave**, subtle but defined contrast between the pink and green patches emphasizes the relationship between the shapes, giving the illusion of diagonal strips across the surface.

①
②
③ **Blossom Time** A flowery, smudged print (1) with light and dark greens and pinks is the focus fabric, while pale pink (2) and green (3), "lifted" from the print, tend to fade into the background, leaving the floral print to provide the main impact.

①
②
③ **Shadowy Stars** Subdued contrast between the darker tone of soft plum (2) and a medium tint of sky blue (3) gives the star shapes a rather shadowy appearance against the very pale tint of green (1) in the background, emphasizing the pattern of large and small green squares.

Cross and Square template This template shows the individual pieces of a block, irrespective of color.

①
②
③ **Poplars** A fresh tint of lime green (2), with its touch of yellow, makes a crisp contrast to the two tones of blue (1, 3) in a color scheme inspired by one of Monet's paintings of poplars in the spring.

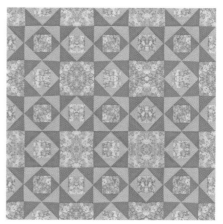

1 **Tartan Weave** Very pale tints of pink (2) and
2 complementary green (3), echoing darker
3 tones in the floral print (1), seem to sink into
the background and join together to weave in
diagonal lines across the surface.

1 **Ambient Warmth** A harmonious marriage of
2 pale tones of shell pink (2) and mauve (3)
3 creates a soft, warm ambience, enhanced by
the addition of soft donkey brown (1). The
main focus is on the brown squares because
they are in a slightly deeper tone than the
other colors.

1 **Rock Pool** A combination of cool, sea green
2 (1) and pale bluish gray (2) gets a touch of
3 warmth from the addition of rose pink (3),
rather like looking at anemones in a rock pool.
A mixture of cool and warm colors, even in
subdued tints, always gives a little vibrancy to
a quilt surface.

1 **Elegant and Restrained** A medium tone of
2 soft coffee brown (2) and a much paler tint of
3 it (3) make a harmonious combination, yet
contrast sufficiently to emphasize the pattern
of squares and stars. Pale, mottled aqua (1)
also provides a pleasing contrast to an
elegant quilt that suits a variety of décors.

tints/**Amish Style**

When strong contrast is used between the center square-on-point and the surrounding triangles, they tend to play the major role in the design, as you can see in **Center Focus** and **Fall Concerto**. Where contrast between the shapes in the center square is less marked, the other large squares tend to come forward, as, for instance, in **Citrus Fruit** and **Speedwell**. In **Mulberry Tree**, which is essentially a harmonious color scheme, the small proportion of pale pink becomes the focus.

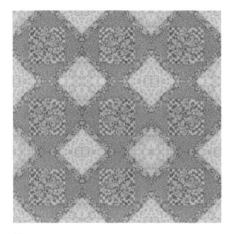

1 **Visual Texture** Subtly patterned fabrics lend
2 a slightly hazy, textured effect to the quilt
3 surface. Pale mauve (2) and blue (4) merge
4 so that the main contrast is between the
peach (3) and pale leaf green (1).

1 **Citrus Fruit** A combination of clean, tangy
2 citrus colors, the slightly stronger orange (3)
3 makes the main impact. Yellow (1) squares
4 outlined by lime green (2) contribute to the
generally crisp, refreshing effect of the
quilt overall.

Amish Style template
This template shows the individual pieces of a block, irrespective of color.

1 **Center Focus** The contrast between medium
2 violet (2) and pale yellow (4), surrounded by
3 green (3), makes the center squares stand
4 out, while the blue (1) squares outlined by
violet, where the contrast is reduced, tend to
recede. This is a quilt inspired by the light,
fresh colors of early spring flowers and leaves.

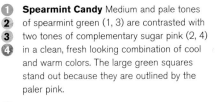

1 **Spearmint Candy** Medium and pale tones
2 of spearmint green (1, 3) are contrasted with
3 two tones of complementary sugar pink (2, 4)
4 in a clean, fresh looking combination of cool
and warm colors. The large green squares
stand out because they are outlined by the
paler pink.

1 **Speedwell** Touches of speedwell blue (4)
2 make a cheerful contribution to a spring-like
3 color scheme without obtruding too much
4 because the blue is juxtaposed with soft,
pale gray (3). Bright yellow (2) outlining green
(1) squares emphasizes the checkerboard
pattern.

1 **Mulberry Tree** Pale (4) and medium (3)
2 tints of mulberry pink harmonize with a light
3 tint of pinkish brown (2), while a slightly
4 darker tone of brown (1) makes an
unobtrusive background to a warm,
comfortable color scheme.

1 **Fall Concerto** Very pale autumnal tints (1, 4)
2 throw into relief the dark tones of russet
3 brown (2) and orange (3), so the main focus
4 is on the slightly brighter orange squares
outlined by brown, giving this harmonious
combination of tints a little extra spice.

tints/**Georgia**

Subsidiary patterns that appear in repeated blocks of Georgia are clearly defined as a series of large octagons surrounded by squares, and smaller octagons containing crosses. But notice that by playing with the arrangement of colors and tints different pattern elements advance or recede. **Pale Reflections**, for instance, seems almost entirely dominated by large octagons, whereas in **Through the Hoops** the squares and crosses are emphasized.

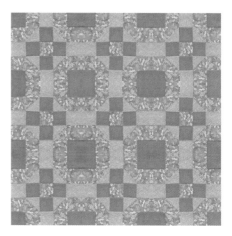

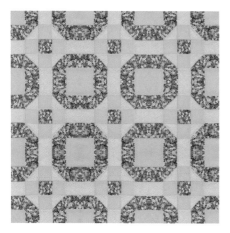

1 **Pale Reflections** Tints of lime green (1) and
2 buttercup yellow (3) are pale reflections of
3 some of the colors in the floral print (2), which, being darker, appears as a series of rings lying over the shapes made by the other colors.

1 **Deep Pools** Mid-blue (1) and a pale tint of
2 aqua (2) form pools across the surface.
3 Contrast with the pale pink (3) gives the blue crosses strong definition. A combination of carefully matched tones of cool blue and green with warm pink creates a quilt that is at once pretty and full of character.

Georgia template
This template shows the individual pieces of a block, irrespective of color.

1 **Rose Borders** A clear pattern of crosses
2 in octagons connected by pink (3) bands
3 dominates the design because the yellow (2) tends to recede into the background behind brown (1) and pink shapes, while still contributing to the generally warm and mellow ambience of the color scheme.

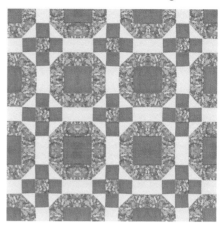

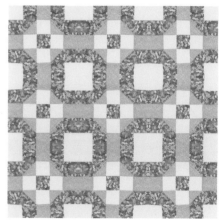

(1) (2) (3) Garland of Lilies A soft tint of dove gray (1) forms a subtle background to garlands of pale lilac (2), which gain added definition when set against medium green (3) with just a hint of blue. The overall effect is calm and relaxing.

(1) (2) (3) Through the Hoops Light coffee brown (2) hoops surround deep blue (1) squares on a very pale primrose (3) background. Because the blue crosses are juxtaposed to pale, complementary yellow they make a very clear statement in the design.

(1) (2) (3) Emerald Islands Two very pale, harmonizing tints of brown (2) and salmon pink (3) tend to merge slightly so the medium emerald green (1) shapes catch the eye first, with the squares and crosses popping out from the surface.

(1) (2) (3) Lemon Squash Cheerful lemon yellow (1) squares and crosses look clean and sharp against complementary violet (2) and pale greenish gray (3) in a cheerful, summery color scheme.

FIVE-PATCH BLOCKS

tints/**Grape Basket**

The simple basket shapes of this block make an excellent canvas for trying out the effects of different colors and combinations. Notice what happens when darker tones are used for the triangles in the center of the baskets, as in **Strawberry Shortcake** and **Contemporary Chic**, where the effect of flying triangles pointing in the same direction is emphasized. When contrast between baskets and background is pronounced, the baskets become the dominant feature, as you can see in **All at Sea** and **Baskets of Violets**.

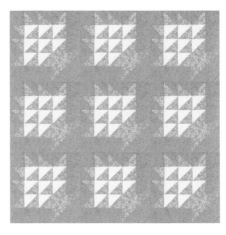

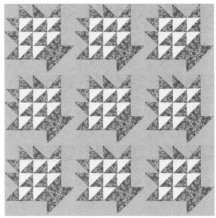

1 2 3 **Sweet Pea Baskets** A pretty floral print (2) incorporates tints that are picked up and echoed in cool, pale aqua (1) in the background and pale mauve (3) in the baskets. Using the aqua in the background enhances the cool, fresh feel of the quilt as it is set against the darker print.

Grape Basket template
This template shows the individual pieces of a block, irrespective of color.

1 2 3 **Spring Weather** A cheerful, uncomplicated color scheme in which a bright, summery tint of yellow (3) looks even brighter against the medium leaf green (2) and complementary sky blue (1).

1 2 3 **Baskets of Violets** The baskets gain definition when the violet (2) shapes are directly juxtaposed to complementary peach (1). Yellow (3) looks extra bright set against medium violet but its proximity to orange on the color wheel gives the scheme unity.

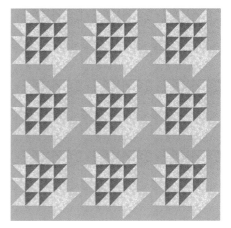

1 **All at Sea** A quilt on a distinctly nautical
2 theme: a subtle tint of aqua (3) harmonizes
3 with a deeper shade of sea-green (2), which
gives the baskets definition as they float on a
pale, ice-blue (1) ocean.

1 **Strawberry Shortcake** Medium pink (3)
2 and pale biscuit brown (2) baskets rest on a
3 pale pink (1) background. The positioning of
the darker pink triangles shows as a
traditional "flying geese" pattern, giving focus
to an otherwise warm, relaxed scheme.

1 **Blue Lagoon** A hint of pink in both the
2 deep lilac blue (1) background and the pale
3 lilac (3) triangles gives the scheme unity
and a touch of warmth, while aqua (2) in
the baskets imparts a generally light,
refreshing atmosphere.

1 **Contemporary Chic** Yellow (2) and brown
2 (3) always looks smart together. Set against
3 a background of elegant turquoise (1) this
scheme looks cool and sophisticated with
a distinctly contemporary air about it.

tints/**Bear's Paw**

Neutral colors for the frames in **Rococo Décor** are so harmoniously matched with the other colors that they enhance the delicate and restrained effect. In **Apricot Windows**, where a stronger tone of a complementary color is used for the frames, they stand out to define the block within them much more assertively. The shapes within the grid acquire greater or lesser definition according to the tones used— they are less obtrusive when the frames are in similar tones to those in the other shapes.

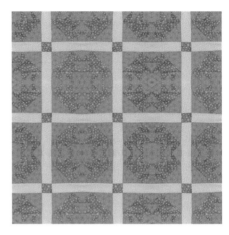

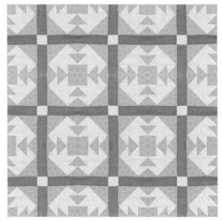

1 **2** **3** **Apricot Windows** Turquoise (2) and apricot (3) are always a popular choice for bed quilts, but can look a little insipid and uninspired. Avoid this by using a very pale tint of the turquoise (1) to act as a neutral, and a brighter tone of peach for the frames.

1 **2** **3** **Rococo Décor** Bluish green (1) makes a subdued background for pale plum (2) in a similar tone, forming a slightly shadowy pattern inside pinkish cream (3) frames. A delicate color scheme inspired by those in rococo décor.

1 **2** **3** **Sashed Windows** Good contrast between the fresh green (1) and pale primrose (2) gives the pattern between the lines of the grid definition. Medium reddish lilac (3) sashes add interest without dominating the pattern in a charming, well-balanced color scheme.

Bear's Paw template
This template shows the individual pieces of a block, irrespective of color.

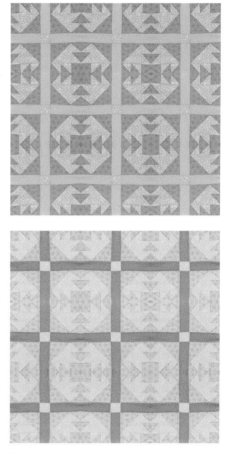

1 **Shrinking Violets** Pale violet (1) next to a
2 soft tint of orange (2) has a little vibrancy,
3 enhanced by the green (3) frames
surrounding the shapes, but contrast between
the orange and green makes the orange look
brighter while the violet tends to recede.

1 **Scotch Mist** Pale taupe (1) matches with
2 sky blue (2) so that the shapes formed
3 within the sashings look like a slightly hazy
landscape seen through green (3) window
frames.

1 **Dusky Pink** Shapes in pale dusky pink (1)
2 and mid-brown (2) lie between bands of
3 neutral cream (3). A very peaceful and
relaxed color scheme with a sense of
harmony and balance.

1 **Faded Pink** Pale lime green (2) is just a
2 touch stronger in tone than the salmon pink
3 (1), which therefore tends to fade into the
background, an effect that is emphasized
because of the slightly stronger contrast
between the green and the smoky mauve (3)
of the sashings.

tints/**Lincoln's Platform**

Placement of dark, medium, and light values gives variation to the graphic effects of even a formal, structured pattern like Lincoln's Platform. In **Tints and Tones**—a classic example of a monochrome scheme—by using a very dark tone for the bands and a very pale tint for the corner patches, a strong effect of layers emerges. In **Lighthearted Mood**, where all the tones are of similar value, the effect is of a simple pattern enclosed within frames.

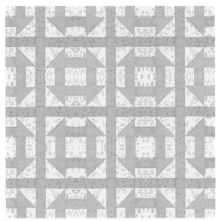

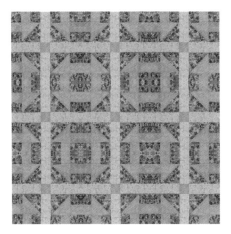

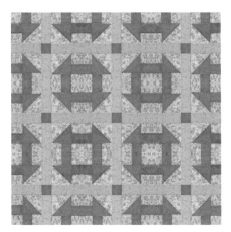

1 2 3 Cooling Down Two very warm pinks (1, 2) blend together harmoniously in a quiet, unobtrusive color scheme that is given a fresh, lively feel by adding cooling aqua blue (3) for the frames.

1 2 3 Dandelions Subtle contrast between dandelion yellow (1) and marigold (2) makes a cheerful combination, the fresh, light effect of the color scheme being enhanced by the addition of a green (3) frame in a slightly deeper tone.

Lincoln's Platform template This template shows the individual pieces of a block, irrespective of color.

1 2 3 Green Gables The pattern inside the frame is well defined by a soft tint of orange (1) and a slightly stronger tone of complementary blue (2). Pale grass green (3) frames give added definition without obtruding too much.

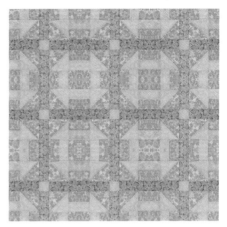

①
2
❸ **Tints and Tones** A classic monochrome color scheme using three blues, medium (1), light (2), and navy (3). A pale tint of blue (2) for the main pattern shapes gives good contrast with the medium blue (1), and using the very dark navy (3) for the frames gives the pattern its layered effect.

1
2
3 **Lighthearted Mood** Sweet spring colors in similar tones have the lighthearted atmosphere of an amusement park. Sunshine yellow (1) and complementary blue (2) ensure that the pattern between the pink (3) frames holds its own.

①
2
3 **Subtle Layers** Subtle contrast between the two mauves, pale (2) and medium (3), used in the frames means that there is a strong visual illusion of layers, with the green (1) appearing as the bottom layer.

1
2
3 **Stepping Stones** Where aqua (2) in a medium tone meets complementary strawberry pink (3) the "posts" where the lines join form a series of focal points across the surface. The greenish yellow (1) background imparts a generally cheerful atmosphere.

tints/**Claws**

Changing the background colors and tones can mean the difference between stars that stand out or recede. In **Hazy View** the stars almost vanish into the similarly toned background, whereas in **Bluebell Wood**, with its clearly defined dark background, the stars stand out brightly. Strong tones in the points around the stars in, for example, **Fuchsia Bush**, draw the eye to the strong diagonal elements of the pattern.

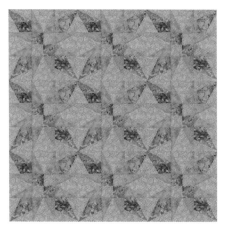

1 2 3 Hazy View Medium tints of lilac (3) and olive (2) have been lifted from the slightly darker floral print (1). Both the lilac and the print tend to disappear into the olive background so the overall effect is subtly soft and hazy.

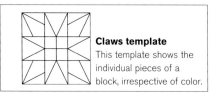

Claws template
This template shows the individual pieces of a block, irrespective of color.

1 2 3 Bluebell Wood A color scheme inspired by woodland bluebells and primroses on a spring morning. Yellow (3), being slightly brighter than the other colors, gives the stars a real sparkle among the green (1) "leaves" and darker blue (2) of the "bluebells."

1 2 3 Tangerine Points The orange (1) patches, being a little brighter than the lilac (2) and blue (3), catch the eye first, so that the diagonal lines moving in both directions across the pattern become the main focus. The orange cross shapes are particularly prominent.

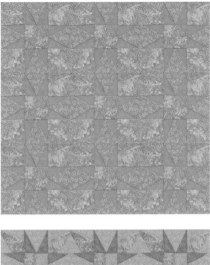

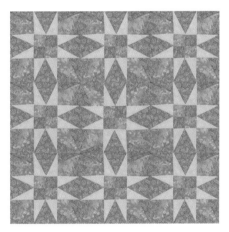

①②③ Cherry Pink Green (3) stars shine out gently from a softly muted background of pale cherry pink (1) and softest donkey brown (2). Contrast between cool green and the warm, harmonious background gives the stars just enough emphasis without spoiling the generally calm overall effect.

①②③ Waters on a Starry Night Cool and elegant, this is a subtle color scheme in which the pretty green (2), with its hint of blue, makes the perfect background to the delicate lilac (1) and deep blue (3) stars. The lilac adds a comforting touch of warmth.

①②③ Fuchsia Bush Pale pink (3) stars surrounded by darker fuchsia pink (1) points echo the shapes of petals set on an emerald green (2) background. Cool and warm contrast adds a little vibrancy to a generally sweet and pretty color scheme.

①②③ Serenity All the colors here are of similar tones; even the creamy yellow (3) of the stars is softly muted so that although it contrasts with the complementary blue (1) and violet (2), the generally calm and serene overall effect is not disturbed.

tints/**Puss in the Corner**

Significant variations on the pattern are achievable by mixing and matching tints and tones. Notice that in **Fair and Square**, for example, the pale pink is of a much brighter value than the other colors, so that those shapes dominates the pattern. In **Decorative Mosaics** the blue and yellow colors are of similar tone and the orange is only a touch darker, so all the shapes have almost equal visual impact, resulting in a cheerful, open design.

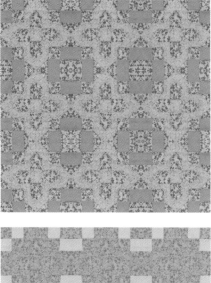

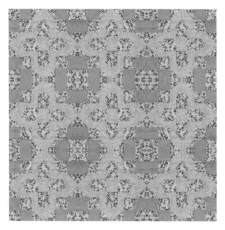

1 2 3 Pastel Clouds Contrast between the pretty floral print (1) and pale greenish aqua (3) is so subdued that the patches merge to form cloud-like shapes, set with rows of pale violet (2) boxes in an unusual combination of colors and visual texture.

1 2 3 Marmalade Crosses The faintly defined pale blue (1) and dove gray (2) shapes form a shadowy background to the brighter marmalade yellow (3), to give those shapes the major role in the design. Maximum effect is gained from juxtaposing blue and complementary orange.

1 2 3 Fair and Square The medium emerald green (1) and lilac (3) are of similar tone, so the contrast between them is subdued. The pale shell pink (2) is much brighter than the other colors, and so focuses the eye on a distinctive pattern of pink squares with green corners to give a light and pretty effect.

Puss in the Corner template This template shows the individual pieces of a block, irrespective of color.

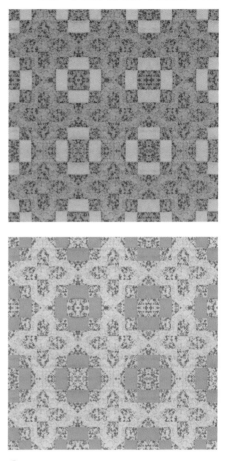

1
2
3
Decorative Mosaics Similar tones of yellow (1) and blue (2) both contrast well with a slightly darker tone of orange (3), giving a cheerful, well-balanced design reminiscent of Victorian wall and floor tile patterns. This color scheme would perfectly complement a room predominantly decorated in cream or white.

1
2
3
Through the Keyhole A background of violet (1) and pale sky blue (2) appear subdued under the bright tone of yellowish green (3). Where green and complementary violet are juxtaposed, the violet patches seem to peep out from within the green crosses.

1
2
3
Orange Boxes Vaguely perceived shapes in greenish gray (1) and blue (3) merge to form a background to the brighter, more assertive orange (2) patches. Using a mottled background of this sort is soft on the eye, and adds interest to the design without drawing too much attention to itself.

1
2
3
Stone Walls Mauvish pink (1) and grayish green (2) shapes separate the pale gray (3) patches, which surround and limit some of the pink shapes. All the shapes and patterns have similar value, creating a calm and subdued design, although the pale gray, being slightly brighter, gives the pattern definition.

EIGHT-POINTED STARS

tints/**Star of the East**

Change the mood and graphic effects of a simple star pattern by mixing and matching colors, tones, and tints. Stars can be bright and sparkly, as in **Blue Yonder**, or cloudy and restrained, as in **Gray Skies. Open Skies** achieves a pretty, fresh effect with a distinctly feminine look to it by contrasting soft pinks with a clear, bright kingfisher blue background, while a more sultry mood is created in **Sunset Stars** by reducing the contrast between stars and background.

1 **2** **3** **Gray Skies** A very calm, subdued color scheme in which misty gray-green (1) forms a gentle background. Pale pinkish lilac (2) picks up on tints in the slightly darker floral print (3), giving the stars an intriguing suggestion of dimension without distracting from the generally soft and harmonious overall effect.

1 **2** **3** **Wild Daffodils** Two tints of daffodil yellow (2, 3) echo the colors of the petals and trumpets of wild-growing daffodils. The stars, lying on a background of glaucous leaf green (1), have a gentle radiance in a very simple but effective color scheme.

Star of the East template This template shows the individual pieces of a block, irrespective of color.

1 **2** **3** **Tinted Green** A medium tone of jade green (2) is matched with a lighter tint (3) of the same, giving the stars a subtly faceted effect that gains added vibrancy when placed on a strong, complementary orange (1) background. The paler tint (3) adds a lighter touch to an otherwise assertive color scheme.

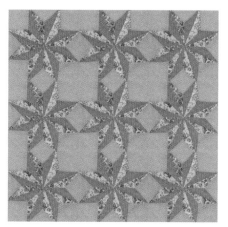

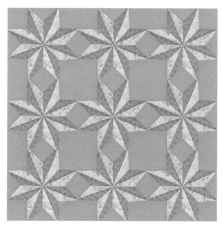

①
②
③
Open Skies Softly faceted stars in pale pink (2) and even paler grayish pink (3) have a fresh, open quality when set on a background of bright kingfisher blue (1), in a quilt with a distinctly feminine touch to it.

①
②
③
Sunset Stars On a soft apricot (1) sky, evoking the colors of sunset, stars in equally soft gray-green (2) and pink (3) look a little shadowy, creating a generally warm and sultry atmosphere. A quilt to enhance a room with a soft, understated décor.

①
②
③
Blue Yonder Pale lavender (2) and yellow (3) contrast well to give the stars plenty of visual impact, but the contrast between the blue (1) and lavender is less pronounced, so the yellow stands out the most clearly.

①
②
③
Simple Elegance Medium tan (2) with palest sage (3) emphasize the faceted effect of the stars, which are set off to advantage on a pale, sky blue (1) background in a dignified, restrained color scheme.

tints/**Virginia Star**

Tints can be effectively mixed and matched with darker and brighter colors, although it's important to choose those that will give the scheme harmony and balance. In **Peach Stones** aqua and orange make an effective contrast, but by choosing peach, a pale version of the orange, for the centers of the stars the colors are drawn together for a well-balanced scheme. In **Shadowy Stars** a similar effect is at work, although here the significantly darker gray of the background makes the stars stand out.

Flowery Haze Pale tints of olive green (2), subdued tones of salmon pink (3) and mauve (4) echo colors in the floral print (1), giving the scheme unity. Using green for the star tips gives them subtle definition against the flowery background, without detracting from the hazy, harmonious ambience of the quilt.

Lemon Points Harmonious tints of blue (1), green (4), and lilac (3) get a real twinkle from the introduction of bright lemon (2) star points, which join to form a pattern of their own across the surface of the quilt.

Peach Stones Strong contrast between the mid-peach background (1) and pale tint of aqua (2) is reinforced by adding a slightly darker tone of aqua (3). Pale peach pink (4) centers echo the background and pull the scheme together.

Virginia Star template
This template shows the individual pieces of a block, irrespective of color.

Rock Pool Medium sea green (1) makes a watery setting for the star-shaped anemones, pieced in colors moving outward from lavender (4) to pale shell pink (3) and a slightly darker pink (2).

Warm Hearts Peach (2) star points tend to fade into the soft chocolate brown (1) background, setting a warm, harmonious tone that is underlined by the pale pink (3) diamonds. Significantly darker pink (4) centers for the stars therefore stand out more strongly and provide focal points.

Chocolate Stars Surrounding chocolate brown (4) center stars with complementary pale aqua (3) gives them the main focus in the design. Pale peachy (2) diamonds are a reflection of the brown centers, but contrast just enough with the pale greenish gray (1) background to have some definition.

Shadowy Stars Subtle shading of pale (2) and slightly darker (3) yellow gives the stars a shadowy dimension. The pale grayish lavender (4) center is echoed by a deeper tone of the same color (1) in the background, drawing the scheme together and at the same time providing a foil for the stars.

tints/**Bow Tie**

All of these quilts retain a light, youthful feel, even though sometimes deeper shades and tones are included to add depth and emphasis. Effective use is also made of the contrast between cool and warm colors. **Cool and Elegant**, for example, mixes cool aqua with a soft pink, but the addition of neutral pearl strikes a balance between the other colors and emphasizes the generally light effect. In **Fresh Focus** this play on the cool/warm theme is used to inject a bright, cheerful note into the more sedate colors.

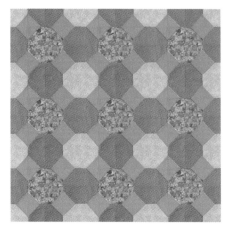

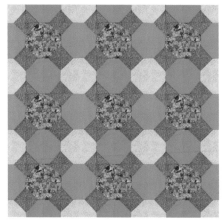

①
②
③
④
Spring Symphony The pretty, spring-like print (4) has a very pale green background, so the octagons pieced in this fabric advance from the other shapes, pieced in tints of tan (1), yellow (2), and lime (3) to echo the colors in the print and create a gentle, harmonious quilt in early spring colors.

Bow Tie template
This template shows the individual pieces of a block, irrespective of color.

①
②
③
④
Cool and Elegant When cool, neutral lilac (1) and mint green (2) are matched with warm peach (3) and pink (4), the result is light and elegant. Octagons in pink and pearl stand out because they contrast well with the green, so the peach shapes appear to form a background to the other colors.

①
②
③
④
Lemon Twist Although proportionately less, the light, bright tone of the yellow (1), contrasting well with a medium tint of grass green (3), catches the eye first and gives a sense of structure and balance to the design. Quiet silvery gray (2) and violet (4) merge slightly to form a subdued background.

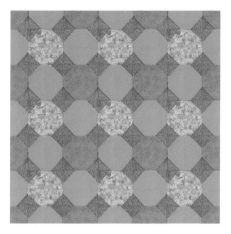

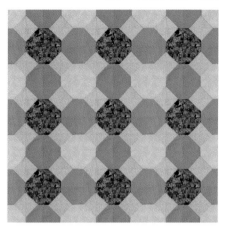

① ② ③ ④ Harmonious Green While peach with green is a popular color choice, tints and tones must be chosen carefully to avoid blandness. Here, two harmonious greens (1, 3), with washed-out blue (4), make a refreshing combination and form the main statement in the quilt. Soft, dusky peach (2) adds a touch of warmth.

① ② ③ ④ Formal Design Pale yellow (3) looks at its brightest against deep purple (2), so that looked at in one way yellow octagons and purple squares appear to create the formal, structured effect of a grid, with pale greeny blue (1) and lilac (4) shapes as a background.

① ② ③ ④ Lacework The network effect is even more pronounced here, where pink (2) squares create a light, airy effect over sky blue (3), with octagons of pale apple green (1) and deep dusky pink (4) giving alternate dark and light focal points.

① ② ③ ④ Fresh Focus Cool eggshell blue (1) creates a series of refreshing focal points when juxtaposed to a harmonious combination of salmon pink (2), donkey brown (3), and pale coffee (4), giving the final effect a cheerful warmth.

tints/**Kaleidoscope**

There is a natural rhythm to Kaleidoscope patterns, which can be emphasized by discreet changes in the placement of colors and tones. Generally speaking, good contrast between the triangles and diamonds is decisive. Notice that in both **Cheerful Outlook** and **Graceful and Stylish** the optical illusion of interlinking circles is more obvious than in **Lighted Windows**, where the patterns are less distinct because contrast between the triangles and diamonds is limited.

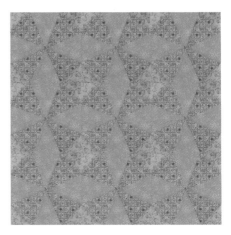

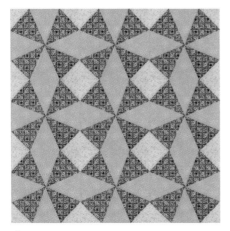

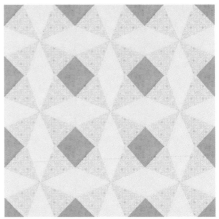

1
2
3 **Tranquility** A suggestion of gray in the formal print (2) is echoed in the pale grayish green (3) creating a calm, tranquil effect. Pale orange (1) squares between the main shapes lift the scheme and avoid any suggestion of somberness without disturbing the generally serene atmosphere.

1
2
3 **Lighted Windows** Shapes pieced in subtly contrasting lilac (2) and blue (3) tend to merge so that the lilac octagons look almost like shadows beneath blue diamonds. The bright orange (1) patches peep out between the shadows like lighted windows.

1
2
3 **Yellow Whirl** The optical illusion of circles is emphasized when light and dark tints of yellow (3, 2) are used together, with apple green (1) squares interspersed between the other shapes to enhance a light, fresh overall effect.

Kaleidoscope template
This template shows the individual pieces of a block, irrespective of color.

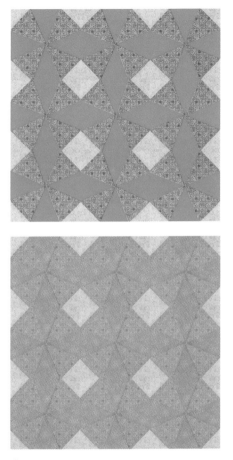

①
②
③
Cheerful Outlook Complementary pink (2) and a stronger tone of aqua (3) look fresh and crisp together, and emphasize the rhythm of the pattern. The addition of a very pale, neutral pearl gray (1) confirms and enhances the generally cool yet cheerful aura of the quilt.

①
②
③
Sweet Spring Colors Very pale dusky pink (1) squares-on-point give added definition to the octagons and diamonds pieced in slightly darker tones of sweet spring colors, apple green (2) and lilac (3), which consequently make a strong pattern across the surface while retaining the light, pretty atmosphere.

①
②
③
Sea and Sand Shapes in a light, bright tone of yellow (2) swirl beneath orange (3) diamonds, with sea green (1) squares peeping through in a very light and lively quilt, evoking memories of a sunny summer's day at the seaside.

①
②
③
Graceful and Stylish Blue (2), with a hint of mauve in it, and light and dark tones of coffee (1, 3) make for a very elegant and tasteful color scheme, at the same time emphasizing the circular rhythm of the pattern. This quilt would make a stylish contribution to a room decorated in cream or blue.

SQUARES IN SQUARES

tints/**Lattice and Square**

The underlying lattice effect of this block is more obvious when contrast between the square patches and surrounding colors is marked. Examples of this can be seen clearly in **Openwork** and **Peppy Peppermint**. Tints can also be used to lift and brighten more subtle and subdued color combinations, such as in **Pink Squares**, where the long rectangles form squares that stand out and become the main focus of the quilt. In **Purple Rain**, tints have a gently subduing effect.

1 **2** **3** **Gold Squares** Although the grayish green (1) background is proportionately greater than the other fabrics, it tends to recede when juxtaposed with the richer, more assertive colors of gold (2) and plum (3). The slightly brighter tone of the gold squares gives them prominence.

Lattice and Square template This template shows the individual pieces of a block, irrespective of color.

1 **2** **3** **Happy-go-lucky** Two pretty pastels, orange (1) and pale green (2), are matched with a deeper tone of lavender (3), which, being complementary to the orange, contrasts well with it and stands out, lending structure and definition to an essentially lighthearted quilt.

1 **2** **3** **Openwork** A medium tint of greeny blue (1) and a lighter, brighter tone of yellow (2) emphasize the lattice effect, which is very slightly disrupted when more somber dove gray (3) squares are added.

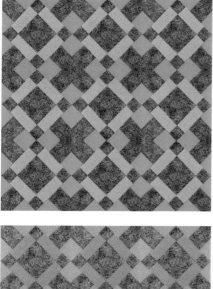

①② ③ Pink Squares Pink (3) squares dominate the scene because they are brighter than the subdued dusky pink (1) patches to which they are juxtaposed, but complementary green (2), also quite bright in tone, peeps out and adds a little resonance to a basically calm and tranquil quilt.

①② ③ Backup Tints Although green (1) is the darker of the three colors, it is also a little brighter than the pale blue (2) and mauve (3), so catches the eye in a series of subtly defined crosses and squares, while the other two colors, which are similar in tone, act as backup.

①② ③ Purple Rain The really strong, vibrant contrast between purple (2) and gold (3) is somewhat modified by the addition of a pale tint of the purple (1), so while the gold "windows" surrounded by purple squares have strong visual impact, the overall effect is very slightly hazy and muted.

①② ③ Peppy Peppermint A strong tint of salmon pink (1) and a medium tone of harmonious brown (3) look mellow and comfortable, and could even be a little bland. However, the bright peppermint (2) squares interspersed between the other shapes give the whole quilt a lift, making it both warm and lively.

tints/**Washington Pavement**

Although various effects emerge when tints are played against stronger or brighter colors, the main impression is usually still quite gentle. Even quilts like **Complementary Tints** and **Raspberry Ripple**, while having plenty of brightness, are dainty and feminine. More subtle and subdued effects are obtained, as in **Calm and Peaceful**, when a tint is matched with slightly darker tones.

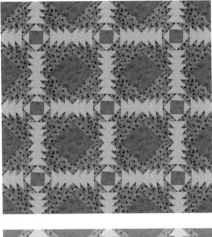

①②③ Feathery Lines There's a slightly autumnal feel to this quilt, with gold (1) squares and triangles separating octagons in beige (2), over which lies a grid of feathery lines made by triangles in a tint of green (3).

①②③ Subdued Emphasis Soft, chalky tints of green (1) and lilac (2) make a gentle, low-key impression and act as a backdrop to the brighter tint of peach (3), which comes forward to give subdued emphasis to the grid structure of the design.

Washington Pavement template This template shows the individual pieces of a block, irrespective of color.

①②③ Complementary Tints Warm pink (1) in a similar tone to the blue (2) emphasizes the pattern of alternating squares-on-point and octagons. Serrated lines in a pale greenish yellow (3) seem to overlie the blue octagons. Since the two colors are opposites on the color wheel, they stand out clearly.

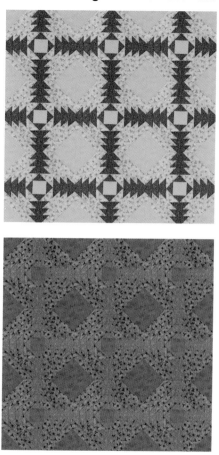

1 **Cheerful Mood** A cheerful, uncomplicated
2 marriage of tints of peach (1) and
3 complementary aqua (3), with a very pale
version of the aqua (2) lying between the
two, emphasizing the light and airy mood
of the quilt.

1 **Raspberry Ripple** A sweet, feminine quilt
2 in which the pale pink (2) octagons form a
3 background for a grid of serrated lines in
deeper raspberry (3), with green (1)
squares peeping out and enhancing the
light, summery ambience.

1 **Quiet Contrast** A soft blue-gray (1) makes
2 a serene background for lilac (2) shapes,
3 against which the lines of green (3) diamonds
in a similar tone show low-key contrast and
confirm the generally gentle and harmonious
overall effect.

1 **Calm and Peaceful** The subdued contrast
2 between slate gray (1) and a soft coffee (2)
3 means that the shapes they make tend to
merge together and sink into the background.
Triangles in equally soft lilac (3), in a similar
tone, lying over the background, enhance the
overall impression of a calm, relaxing quilt.

tints/**Winding Ways**

Winding Ways quilts often confuse the eye as it tries to decide between positive and negative shapes and spaces. This is most obvious when the petal shapes are laid on a paler background, as seen in **Enigmatic** and **Shape and Movement**, where tints are used for the background colors, giving a pleasing dynamism. There is less ambiguity in **Dove Gray Harmony** because, although contrast between the two colors is sufficient to define the shapes, the brighter tone of the petals gives them prominence.

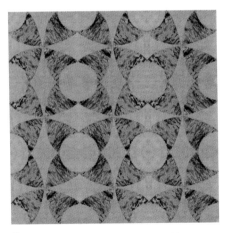

1 **2** **Classic Style** Gold (1) and aqua (2) are a classic a combination when a cool, elegant effect is required. In this quilt, the mainly aqua print in which the petal shapes are pieced contains a touch of gold, so when placed against the gold background the effect is quite muted.

Winding Ways template
This template shows the individual pieces of a block, irrespective of color.

1 **2** **Enigmatic** A very pale tint of shell pink (1) and a slightly deeper tone of sea green (2) produce a fresh looking quilt in which all the patches are clearly defined, so sometimes the pink shapes seem to predominate, sometimes the green.

1 **2** **Mellow Touch** A pale tint of cream (1) has a mellowing touch of sandy beige in it, so when set with sky blue (2) petals shapes the overall effect is very slightly subdued, although the quilt retains its pleasing sense of rhythm and movement.

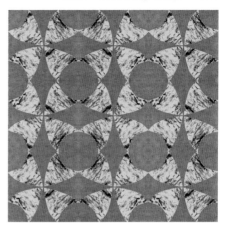

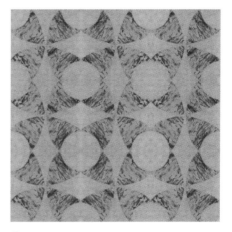

(1) (2) Dove Gray Harmony A dove gray (1) background for a pretty tint of pinkish lilac (2) creates a gentle, harmonious mood. There is sufficient contrast between the two fabrics to define the shapes, but the slightly brighter tone of the lilac shapes mean that they stand out across the surface.

(1) (2) Shape and Movement Medium violet (2) petals set on a background in a delicate tint of mint green (1) look wonderfully fresh and lively, again emphasizing the visual stimulation and movement in this pattern.

(1) (2) Euphorbia Polychroma A garden-inspired color scheme in which bright acid yellow (2) heads of euphorbia make the first impact as they glow out from an intense leaf green (1), although the green shapes are also a strong feature of the design.

(1) (2) Pastel Quilt Similar tones of peach (I) and lilac (2) give maximum effect to all the shapes that appear when blocks are repeated, but despite the lively rhythm of the pattern the pastel colors ensure that this is a gentle, pretty quilt.

tints/**Round Table**

All of these quilts have a pleasingly fresh, lighthearted feel. In some of the quilts, such as **Primrose Buttons** and **Lively Character**, the background shapes have been pieced in complementary colors, which gives them strong definition. However, the overall character of the quilt can be modified by the choice of fabric for the circles. In **Gray Circles**, for example, the circles have a slightly calming effect, while in **Lively Character** they act as bright focal points and lift the whole mood.

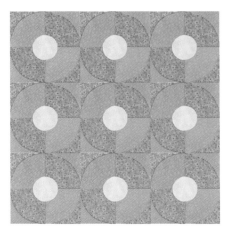

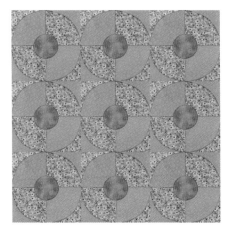

1 Herb Garden A floral print (1) sets the mood
2 for a graceful, harmonious quilt based on tints
3 of lilac (2) found in the print and echoed in the other fabric. Soft spearmint (3) circles also echo the colors in the print, so making a series of toning accents across the surface.

1 Primrose Buttons Well-balanced tones of
2 mint green (1) and complementary rose pink
3 (2) make a fresh, lively combination, given added brightness by primrose yellow (3) "buttons."

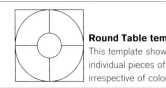

Round Table template
This template shows the individual pieces of a block, irrespective of color.

1 Rose Arbor Tints of blue-gray (1) and aqua
2 (2) make a harmonious background for the
3 bright rosy pink (3) circles, which stand out as strong focal points. The quilt gets even more impact from the warm/cool contrast between the pink and the other colors.

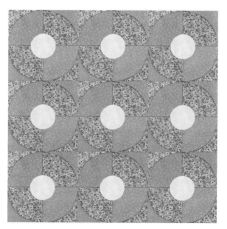

1. **Orange and Apple** Orange (1) and apple
2. green (2) make a pleasing impression, even
3. though the orange is in a slightly deeper tone
   than the green. Adding lemon (3) circles,
   which harmonize with the orange, enhances
   the fresh and invigorating mood of the quilt.

1. **Grace and Favor** Misty gray (1) and lilac (2)
2. combine to create a tranquil background to a
3. very slightly subdued tint of acid green (3),
   which serves to enliven the surface without
   dominating it, so the overall effect is still
   gentle and graceful.

1. **Gray Circles** A fresh tint of green (1)
2. contrasts well with pale salmon pink (2),
3. giving a cool, crisp look to the surface.
   Dove gray (3) circles tone down that effect
   just a little, but the result remains light and
   clean-cut.

1. **Lively Character** Tints of lilac (1) and
2. orange (2) are juxtaposed for clear, strong
3. visual impact. Pale bright yellow (3) also
   contrasts well with the other colors, so
   enhances and exaggerates the clean, lively
   character of the quilt.

tints/**Japanese Fan**

Color schemes based on tints can be surprisingly strong and lively, especially when complementary colors are used to maximize the effect of contrast. **Fair Weather Fans** is a perfect example of this, with complementary blue and orange giving added emphasis to a bright and cheerful scheme. In **Broken Harmony**, dark/light contrast between the fans and backgrounds makes for a strong scheme with a touch of drama, while in **Clear Outline** a bright background determines the quilt's overall fresh, crisp character.

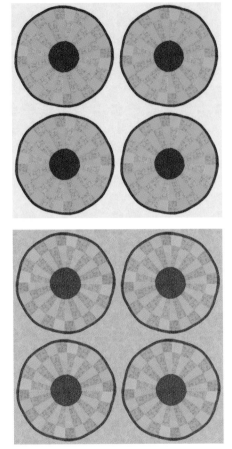

1. 2. 3. 4. **Fair Weather Fans** Fans pieced in softened tints of sunny orange, medium (2) and pale (3), are set on a background of sky blue (1), which is complementary to the orange. Dark blue (4) circles and rims are used to highlight and define the fan shapes and add to the graphic impact of the complementary colors.

1. 2. 3. 4. **Clear Outline** Pale tints of apple green (2) and rose pink (3) give good contrast and definition to the fans. Set on the pale daffodil yellow (1) background, the effect could be too bland and merely pretty, but this is overcome by adding brown (4) rims and circles to strengthen and darken the design.

1. 2. 3. 4. **Gentle and Discreet** Fans in slightly chalky tints of purplish gray (2) and shell pink (3) are set on a neutral cream (1) background. Pinkish brown (4) rims and circles give clear definition between fans and background, but the overall effect is quite gentle and discreet.

Japanese Fan template
This template shows the individual pieces of a block, irrespective of color.

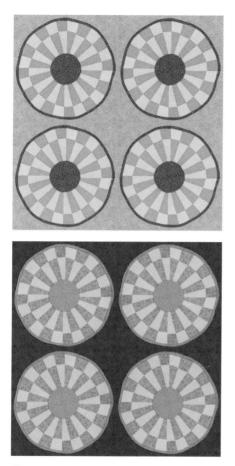

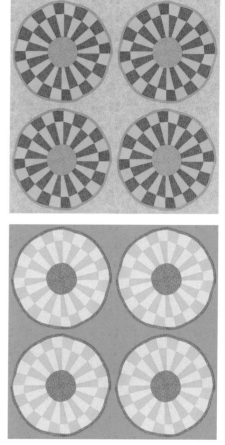

1 **Soothing Combination** Two pale, pretty
2 tints, pink (2) and sea blue (3), are set against
3 two more somber colors, cool gray (1) and
4 donkey brown (4), combining to make a quilt
with a relaxed and soothing atmosphere.

1 **Broken Harmony** Pale salmon (2) and
2 cyclamen (3) set on a deeper plum (1)
3 background make a harmonious combination,
4 but the addition of a touch of bright jade
green (4), which looks jewel-bright in contrast
to the plum, interrupts the harmony and
creates a stronger, more dynamic effect.

1 **Double Harmony** A very pale tint of apple
2 green (2) and a deeper tone of emerald green
3 (3) form a harmonizing combination. When set
4 against two other harmonizing colors, pale
gray (1) and pinkish lilac (4), the effect is soft
and understated, although contrast between
the greens gives the pieced fans definition.

1 **Bright and Lively** Lime (2) and lemon (3)
2 tints are full of light and vigor, an effect
3 emphasized when they are set on a fresh sea
4 blue (1) "sky." The olive (4) circles and rims
tone down the effect just enough to avoid any
suggestion of glare.

FAN BLOCKS

tints/**Friendship Fan**

The pattern made by Friendship Fans when they are repeated and rotated is full of life and movement, and when light, bright tints are applied the result always looks vital and youthful. Look, for example, at **Chocolate Drops**, with its refreshing green and yellow combination, or **Fresh Lemons**, where the brighter value of the yellow lightens the whole surface of the quilt. More subtle effects, though still light and pleasing, appear when harmonious colors are used in the fans, as in **Blended Fans**.

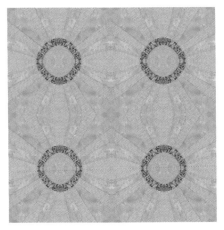

1 **Floral Rings** Delicate pastel tints of rosy
2 pink (1) and palest aqua (2) look fresh and
3 pretty, with circles in a deeper floral print (3) serving as focal points and to give a little depth to the design.

1 **Chocolate Drops** Lime (1) and yellow (2),
2 which are close to each other on the color
3 wheel, make a harmonious combination, but a brighter value for the yellow provides contrast and makes them look quite jaunty. The addition of chocolate (3) rings puts the finishing touch to a tasteful, stylish scheme.

1 **Gentle Touch** The contrast between a
2 medium tone of sea green (1) and a very
3 pale tint of salmon pink (2) gives the fan blades strong definition, and pale rainy gray (3) rings add the gentlest touch of restraint to the scheme.

Friendship Fan template This template shows the individual pieces of a block, irrespective of color.

1
2
3
Cool Tints, Warm Focus Medium tints of mint green (1) and sky blue (2) combine to make very cool and harmonious fans, while the lilac (3) rings add variety and a little warmth in a series of focal points.

1
2
3
Vibrant Tints Similar tones of jade green (1) and complementary pink (2) look quite vibrant together and create a strong impression, so smoky blue (3) rings are added to provide restful focal points without detracting from the graphic impact of the quilt.

1
2
3
Blended Fans A very subdued color scheme in which pale rose (1) blends softly with cream (2) to make pretty, delicate fans. Green (3), which is a little brighter than the pink, and complementary to it, adds a lively touch without disturbing the light and gentle overall effect.

1
2
3
Fresh Lemons Contrast between pale acid lemon (1) and a softer tone of bluish gray (2) results in clear, bright fans, but cool medium gray (3) rings, being closer in tone and hue to the blue, reduce the impact of the contrast between the two main colors just a little.

tints/**Bleeding Hearts**

The built-in sense of rhythm and movement in the patterns formed is enhanced when color schemes based on tints are used to emphasize different elements. For example, compare **Background Movement** and **Coral Island**, where the square shapes come forward, with **Orange Blossom** and **Fascinating Complexity**, in which circles catch the eye first. The different effects are achieved by careful placement and juxtaposition of dark and light fabrics, but the overall effect is always light and feminine.

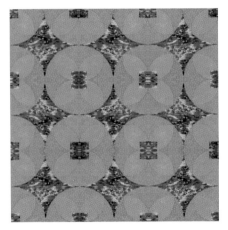

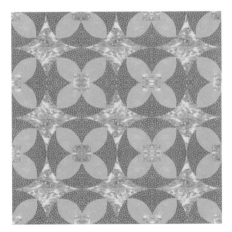

1 2 3 **Tinted Echoes** Pink (2) petal shapes on a medium tint of emerald green (3) catch the eye first. These colors in turn echo tints found in the smudgy floral print (1), which gives the whole design a sense of unity and balance.

1 2 3 **Background Movement** Small squares and the larger curve-sided squares in very bright daffodil yellow (1) come forward strongly from the shapes pieced in soft sage green (2) and pale pinkish lilac (3), which tend to retreat to form a subdued background and contribute a suggestion of movement.

1 2 3 **Tinted Pink Harmony** Shapes in a delicate combination of palest eau-de-Nil (1) and shell pink (2) gain maximum impact from being placed on a background in soft, dusky pink (3), which is just deep enough to let the other colors come forward, the two pinks creating a gently harmonious overall effect.

Bleeding Hearts template This template shows the individual pieces of a block, irrespective of color.

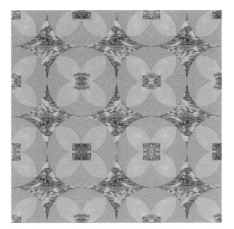

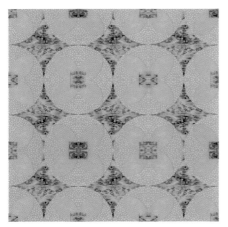

1 2 3 Coral Island Coral (1) squares definitely catch the eye when set on a sea of cool, blended blue (2) and aqua (3). The brighter and warmer tone of the coral, contrasted with the complementary background, gives the quilt a very lively atmosphere.

1 2 3 Orange Blossom Pink (3) circles, surmounted by pale orange (2) petal shapes, are the main focus here, with well-contrasted squares in bright grass green (1) peeping out between them to create a striking color scheme that plays on the warm/cool contrast between the circles and the background.

1 2 3 Fascinating Complexity Although the very pale lilac (1) shapes come forward, there is enough contrast between the dusky pink (2) and mint green (3) to give them equal visual impact, resulting in a fascinatingly complex quilt that is also cool and elegant.

1 2 3 Contrast and Harmony When pale acid yellow (1) shapes are set against a harmonious background pieced in very delicate pinkish lilac (2) and a slightly deeper tint of lilac (3), to which yellow is complementary, the small squares and larger curve-sided squares float over the surface.

APPLIQUÉ BLOCKS

tints/**Dutch Tulips**

The pretty flower shapes made by repeated Dutch Tulips blocks offer a simple but effective way of creating a series of quilts on a floral theme. One way to enhance that theme is to use color schemes based on pastel colors and tints. Yet each quilt here has its own character, and emphasis can be placed on different elements. In **Perfect Balance** and **Floral Dance**, emphasis is on a balanced arrangement of the floral motifs, while in **Pink Lanterns** and **Smart and Stylish** the background has a major influence on the design.

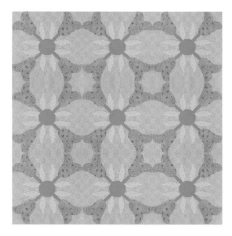

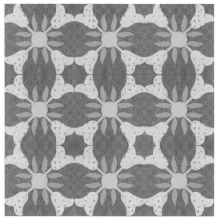

①②③④ Sunny Garden Soft orange (4) suns, surrounded by deep green (3) leaf shapes, shine brightly when set on a pale green (1) background. The shapes pieced in soft, toning blue floral (2) fabric tend to disappear into the background, leaving the orange shapes to make a splash.

Dutch Tulips template
This template shows the individual pieces of a block, irrespective of color.

①②③④ Pink Lanterns Pale sugar pink (1) shapes emerge strongly and form the familiar lantern shapes. Florets in aqua (4) and egg-shell blue (3) are harmonious and gain in value by being placed on the complementary pink background. Bluish lilac (2) flower heads contribute to the soft, gentle atmosphere.

①②③④ Smart and Stylish Square shapes in bright, sharp lemon yellow (2) definitely take center stage when set against soft donkey brown (1), but the blue (3) and pale lime (4) florets set between them have enough impact to balance the pattern in a very smart and stylish quilt.

1 2 3 4 **Pale Peach Focus** Pale and medium tints of peach (3, 2), combined with a soft grayish brown (1), make a warm, harmonious quilt in which contrast is provided by brightening the peach in the florets. Soft, chalky lilac (4) gives tasteful color variation without obtruding too much.

1 2 3 4 **Perfect Balance** A bright lemon (1) background is the perfect foil for rose pink (2) squares which alternate with flower shapes pieced in two harmonizing colors, eau-de-Nil (3) and sea green (4). The tints and tones are perfectly balanced to enhance a quilt with a light, youthful air to it.

1 2 3 4 **Floral Dance** All of the shapes have equal value and dance across the surface when violet (2) squares alternate with flowers in apple green (3) and medium pink (4). The very pale lilac pink (1) serves as a sympathetic background and enhances the sense of unity and balance.

1 2 3 4 **Delphiniums** Flower shapes in a very pale tint of delphinium blue (3) and a darker tint (4) of the same hue make the most impact against the background of pale lime (1), although alternating squares in peach (2) also make an impression and help to balance the scheme.

Shades

When black is added
to a color, the resulting
darker values of that color are
known as shades. In general, shades
are quiet and sober, and are the ideal
choice for warm, hard-wearing quilts, or situations
where the prevailing mood required is calm and
sedate. Bright values added to shades can also
make quite a dramatic impact.
If a color scheme based on shades looks too
sombre, try adding a very small proportion
of a lighter fabric which may be just
enough to lift the surface.

FOUR-PATCH BLOCKS

shades/**Cross and Square**

When the triangles surrounding the center square merge together, as in **Vanishing Act** and **Sober and Dignified**, you will find that the stars disappear almost completely, becoming part of a straightforward arrangement of joining squares. In **Warp and Weft**, a shadowy pattern of diagonal lines emerges when harmonious colors and shades merge together and the pattern they make is thrown up by juxtaposing them to triangles in a much paler value.

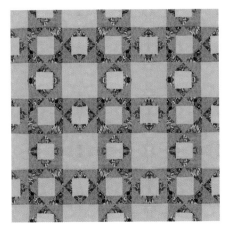

1 2 3 Vanishing Act Patches in a medium shade of turquoise (2) merge with those in a blue print (3), so that an overall pattern of joined squares and rectangles on a slightly brighter yellow (1) background emerges. The stars have disappeared because the turquoise and the blue are of similar tones.

1 2 3 Milk Chocolate Neutral beige (2) against a background of soft chocolate brown (1) sets the tone for a quilt with a gentle, subdued mood, enlivened just enough by the addition of a smaller proportion of a medium shade of violet (3).

1 2 3 Warp and Weft Dark brown (1) and a medium shade of leaf green (2) are juxtaposed with a very pale beige (3), creating a very harmonious overall effect. The two darker colors merge and appear as a subtle pattern of shadowy bands weaving diagonally across the quilt.

Cross and Square template This template shows the individual pieces of a block, irrespective of color.

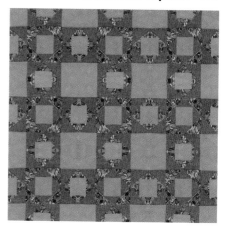

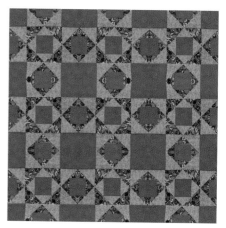

1 2 3 Gold Squares A rich shade of deep lavender (2) for the stars is juxtaposed to a brighter tone of old gold (1) in the background, emphasizing the pattern of gold squares. Pale lilac (3) acts as a neutral because it is lighter in value than the other colors, serving to highlight the stars and surrounding shapes.

1 2 3 Cool Stars Cool looking stars of a very light gray-green (2) are a pale reflection of the medium shade of sea green (3) surrounding them, well set off by being placed on an amethyst (1) background, which gives a touch of warmth to a nonetheless surprisingly fresh looking quilt.

1 2 3 Sober and Dignified The decidedly masculine air of this quilt could appear a little somber, but the slate gray (2) is mitigated by the addition of a touch of mid-brown (3) in the print, and both shades are lifted by the slightly brighter tone of tan brown (1), so the final effect is pleasantly sober and dignified.

1 2 3 Royal Blue Deep royal blue (1) and jade green (2) look rich and glowing together, although the deep blue tends to recede behind the slightly brighter jade green. The glowing effect is subtly enhanced by using a small proportion of a pinkish brown print (3) for contrast.

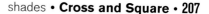

shades/**Amish Style**

Using shades in Amish Style illustrates perfectly the versatility of even simple blocks, from which a wide range of moods and effects can be created. Compare **Seascape**, which is misty and laid-back, creating a lovely soft mood, with the warm, fiery effect of **Stormy Sunset**. When a distinctly brighter tone is used for the center squares, as in **Touch of Pink** and **Purple Passion**, the quilt acquires a lively, more assertive character.

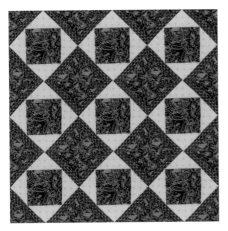

❶❷❸❹ Rich and Dark A floral print in deep aqua (1) is juxtaposed to two prints in deepest burgundy, one floral (2) and the other more formal (4), a combination that is rich in both color and texture, resulting in a complex design highlighted by pale, neutral stone (3).

❶❷❸❹ Touch of Pink Shades of royal blue (1) and grassy green (3) are surrounded by the textured dark gray print (2), giving the squares added definition. The pink (4) centers give a series of bright focal points and add a touch of warmth.

❶❷❸❹ Formal Elegance Subdued shades of brown (1) and tan (4) are soft and could even be bland, but with textured mauve (2) outlines for the very pale brown (3) squares, the final effect is formal and elegant.

Amish Style template
This template shows the individual pieces of a block, irrespective of color.

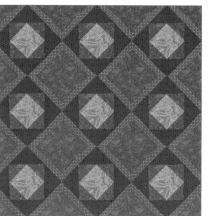

① ② ③ 4 Purple Passion A deep shade of purple (1) sets the tone for a warm, harmonious scheme, enhanced by soft purplish blue (2) and pink (3). Squares in a much paler tone of blue (4) pop out to add a little light relief.

① ② ③ ④ Seascape Misty gray (1) sets a cool tone when juxtaposed to a deep turquoise floral print (2) and navy blue (3). The textured print in a slightly brighter shade of turquoise (4) outlines the squares and adds some textural interest.

① ② ③ ④ Stormy Sunset Ruby red (1) squares are surrounded by deep violet (3), then bands of a textured gray print (2). Soft gray (4) center squares add a necessary light touch without detracting from the hot and fiery overall effect.

① ② ③ ④ Forest Fire Shady leaf green (1) and fiery orange (3) are juxtaposed to emphasize the green squares, the effect being slightly muted by outlining the squares in soft brown (2). Deep pink (4) in the centers of the squares enhance the fiery effect.

shades/**Georgia**

Changing positions of colors and tones sometimes makes it difficult to believe that these are all the same block. Strong contrast between corner patches and center sashings, as seen in **Dusky Pinks** and **Golden Trellis**, reveals a grid pattern of small octagons at the intersections, while in **Hoop-la**, when similar tones are used for all the shapes, a regular pattern of large and small octagons appears.

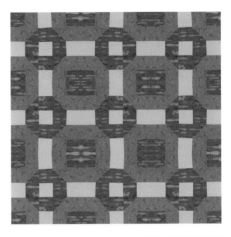

❶
❷
❸
Aquarium In this monochrome scheme a watery pattern on a blue print (1) forms squares and small octagons between navy blue (2) octagons set on a medium aqua (3). The result is cool and dark with subtle glimpses of light catching the ripples in the blue print.

❶
❷
❸
Dusky Pinks Dark, dusky pink (2) appears as a background to deep blue (1) octagons and squares connected by much paler pink (3) rectangles, which dominate the scheme because they are significantly brighter than the other patches.

Georgia template
This template shows the individual pieces of a block, irrespective of color.

❶
❷
❸
Ring O' Roses A harmonious combination of brownish pink (1) and brown (3) forms a pattern of octagons and rectangles against a sky blue (2) background, which injects a cheerful note into a calm, relaxed color scheme.

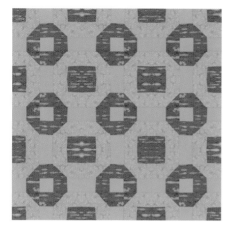

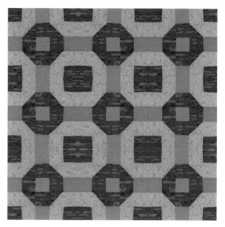

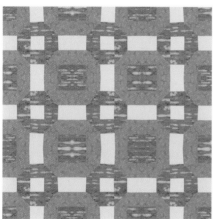

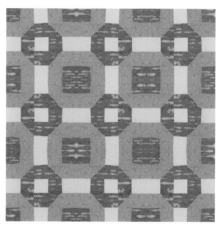

1 2 3 **Hoop-la** Greenish gold rings (2) alternate with smaller shady plum (1) rings, through which medium aqua (3) squares peep out. Similar tones of the colors in the rings give them equal visual impact, while the aqua adds a lively, contrasting touch without obtruding too much.

1 2 3 **Quiet Elegance** Contrast between tea brown (1) and muted pink (2) is subdued so that contrast between those colors and the much brighter tone of neutral cream (3) is emphasized, enlightening a quietly elegant color scheme.

1 2 3 **Orange Squash** Shades of navy blue (1) and pine green (3) are a foil for the much brighter orange (2) octagons, making them the main focus, although the small blue octagons gain some impact by being directly juxtaposed to the complementary orange shapes.

1 2 3 **Golden Trellis** Always a stylish combination, tan brown (1) and golden yellow (3) gain even more impact when set against a background of complementary blue (2). The slightly brighter tone of the yellow brings the rectangle shapes into sharp focus.

shades/**Grape Basket**

A classic basket block can easily assume different guises and moods, such as clear and crisp when the baskets are set against a neutral background, as in **Classic Style**, or dense and opulent when richly colored baskets are set into an equally exotic background, for example in **Purple Grapes**. Maximum visual impact is gained when strong contrast is used within the baskets themselves, as you can see in **Lilac Shadows** and **Complementary Attraction**.

① ② ③ Purple Grapes Shades of rich golden brown (2) and complementary purple (3) have been lifted from a dark print (1) used for the background, against which the baskets of grapes glow harmoniously in a dense and opulent color scheme.

Grape Basket template
This template shows the individual pieces of a block, irrespective of color.

① ② ③ Vine Leaves Dark and pale shades of purple (2, 1) combine harmoniously, but with strong contrast between the pale background and dark triangles in the baskets. Triangles of shadowy leaf green (3) provide contrast and added interest to a very calm and elegant color scheme.

① 2 ③ Complementary Attraction Although the green (1) and complementary pink (3) triangles are separated by a neutral cream (2), they still work together to give strong graphic impact, the overall effect being crisp and stimulating.

①
②
③ **Purple Geese** Harmonious baskets pieced in pale lilac (2) and a deep shade of purple (3) achieve maximum impact when the pale triangles are juxtaposed with the mid-tan (1) background, over which they seem to float. The purple triangles emphasize the "flying geese" formation.

1
②
③ **Classic Style** A rich, deep shade of mauvish brown (2) looks smart and stylish when set with brighter golden olive green (3). A background of very pale green (1) is all that is required to set off the baskets in a classically stylish color scheme.

①
②
③ **Opulence** A bold and striking color scheme in which purple (2) and red (3) baskets look opulent together, an effect that is enhanced because the purple triangles are directly juxtaposed to a greenish gold (1) background.

①
2
③ **Lilac Shadows** Shadowy lilac (1) is a harmonious background to the pale shell pink (2) of the baskets. Deep green (3) triangles, strongly contrasting with the other colors, add a crisp note to an otherwise gentle, restrained color scheme.

shades/**Bear's Paw**

Color schemes based on shades can demonstrate the great versatility and design potential of a simple block like Bear's Paw. Choose between the pale, laid-back effect of **Layered Look**, the strikingly deep and dramatic look of **Orange Bars**, or the understated effect of **Fuzzy Bear**, where the contrast in the "paw" pattern is muted. A comfortable, homely mood is evoked by **Country Style**, in which pattern and colors work perfectly together to create a classic example of a traditional patchwork quilt.

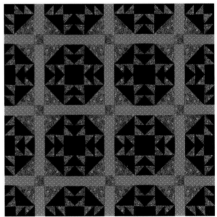

①②③ Country Style Similar tones of golden tan (1), blue (2), and rust (3) give all elements of the pattern equal impact, although the tan shapes, being a touch lighter, tend to come forward. The use of small prints gives added visual texture to an eminently practical, homely color scheme.

①②③ Layered Look Shades of bluish purple (1) and greenish gray (2) appear as blocks lying under a grid of much paler lilac (3), which, being of a significantly brighter tone, dominates the other colors and gives the whole scheme a light and slightly ethereal look.

①②③ Orange Bars A very dramatic yet well-balanced scheme in which contrast between black (1) and mid-olive (2) alone makes for strong impact, but when the blocks are seen below the brighter tone of orange (3) used for the bars, the dramatic effect is heightened.

Bear's Paw template
This template shows the individual pieces of a block, irrespective of color.

❶❷❸ Pink Squares Soft air-force blue (3) outlines a well-defined pattern of harmonious shades of pinkish lilac (2) and brown (1). There is sufficient contrast between the pink and blue to point up the pink squares where the two colors meet.

❶❷❸ Green Outlook A bright, grassy green (3) frames the blocks, in which a medium shade of purple (1) contrasts strongly with the neutral greenish cream (2), giving unity to a fresh, crisp looking color scheme.

❶❷❸ Fuzzy Bear Slate gray (1) and jade green (2) for the "paw" patches tend to merge and become faint beneath the stronger blue (3) of the grid. The green, however, shows up well when it is juxtaposed to the blue, revealing the square shapes under the intersections of the grid.

❶❷❸ Shady Harmony Two shades used for the "paws," cerise pink (1) and deep slatey blue (2), merge and almost disappear beneath the pale lilac (3) grid, although blue squares at the intersections give a series of focal points in a very subtle, understated color scheme.

shades/**Lincoln's Platform**

The long patches at the center of Lincoln's Platform can make a striking difference to the finished effect. In **Crosspatches**, for example, they are pieced in neutral cream, which stands out almost starkly against the shades used for the other patches. In **Pink Latticework** they act as subdued focal points on the lacy background, while in **Brown Study** they appear to join up and form a grid across the surface.

① **Crosspatches** Shades of smoky blue (1)
② and maroon (2) form a subdued background
3 to a series of crisp, bright crosses in neutral cream (3) in a most striking and unusual color scheme with a distinctly contemporary look to it.

Lincoln's Platform template This template shows the individual pieces of a block, irrespective of color.

① **Autumn Forest** Forest green (3) crosses
② give a distinct zing to the autumnal brown (1)
③ and orange (2). The usual pattern of Churn Dash blocks is almost invisible because the brown patches appear isolated on the brighter orange background.

① **Bright Aqua** The cloudy gray (3) frames
② outline a pattern of deep blue (2) and mid-
③ aqua (1), emphasis being on the squares and rectangles in aqua, because it is significantly brighter than the other colors, making this a cool, understated scheme.

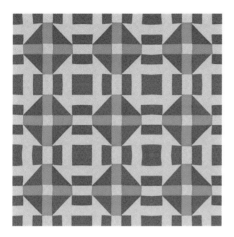

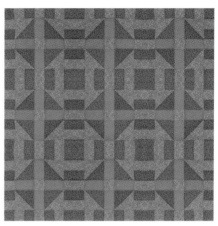

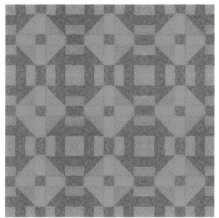

1
2
3 **Light and Bright** Deep blue (1) and complementary orange (3) are a cheerful combination and tend to dominate the scheme, but the larger proportion of neutral gray (2) imparts a generally light, clean look to the quilt.

1
2
3 **Pink Latticework** Although the shady pink (2) is only a touch brighter than the other two colors, it is enough to emphasize the pink shapes, which are seen as a network of lines regularly interrupted by on-point squares in gray (1), set with olive green (3) crosses.

1
2
3 **Brown Study** A warm, monochrome scheme in which shades of burnt orange (2) and brown (1) make a subtle background to brighter, rust-colored (3) crosses lying on brown squares. This scheme would work perfectly in a room with a plain cream or beige décor.

1
2
3 **Gingham Cloth** An illusion of joined lines is created by strong contrast between the pale pink (1) and burgundy (2), the pattern interrupted at intervals by green (3) crosses that contrast with the pink, giving a fresh, clean look to the pattern, reminiscent of gingham cottons.

shades/**Claws**

Shades married to pale tints, as in **Starbright**, can't fail to look bright and cheerful, although a more subdued but still effective color scheme is achieved when shades are placed on a muted background, as in **Greensleeves**. The corner points on the stars assume greater or lesser importance in the design depending on the contrast with the background; for example, in **Cross Currents** the green patches are emphasized, whereas in **Focus on Blue** the paler brown shapes merge into the background.

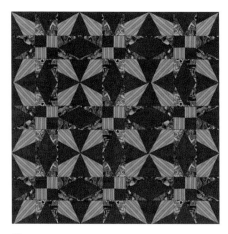

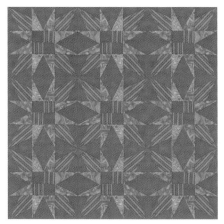

❶❷❸ Cross Currents Deepest burgundy (1) and lighter green (2) echo colors in the mottled print (3) of the stars so closely that the star fabric almost disappears. The shapes pieced in green, being the brightest, dominate the pattern and reveal a strong diagonal bias to the design.

❶❷❸ Midnight Stars Limited contrast between golden olive (1) and soft orange (2) give the dark midnight blue (3) stars the central role in the design. The orange shapes tend to come forward slightly because blue and orange are complementary to each other, giving added intensity to those elements of the pattern.

❶❷❸ Ultramarine Sparkle By contrast with the pink (1) of the background and medium brown (2) of the points in the corners of the stars, the ultramarine (3) stars positively glow. The warm/cool combination of colors heightens this effect in a star quilt with a sparkle.

Claws template
This template shows the individual pieces of a block, irrespective of color.

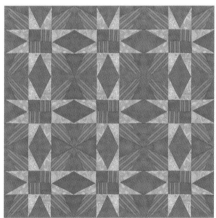

1 **2** **3** **Greensleeves** Deep, shady green (2) next to complementary brick red (3) in a lighter tone ensures maximum impact between the two colors, just slightly modified by the neutral stone gray (1) background, resulting in a quilt that is easy on the eye but with lively splashes of color across the surface.

1 **2** **3** **Welsh Poppies** The lovely purplish blue (1) of violas growing beside complementary soft orange (3) of Welsh poppies inspired this color scheme. Jade green (2) "leaves" make their own subtle contribution to the garden theme, although the brighter tone of the orange stars make them the main focus.

1 **2** **3** **Focus on Blue** Warm orange tan (1) and golden brown (2) are a foil for the royal blue (3) stars, which are brightest when juxtaposed to the complementary orange. Muted contrast between the corner patches of the stars and the background means that they tend to disappear and assume only a supporting role.

1 **2** **3** **Starbright** Clear and fresh, the pale primrose yellow (1) is a perfect backdrop to the complementary blue (2) and burnt orange (3) in the stars. The orange and blue are of similar tone so both stand out equally against the background, underlining the generally bright and cheerful effect.

NINE-PATCH BLOCKS

shades/**Puss in the Corner**

Color schemes based on shades are perfect for creating warm, homely quilts like **Touch of Scarlet** and **Olive Grove**. Matched with brighter colors, shades can also produce more striking graphic effects, as in **Bright Outlook**, where the pale lavender "windows" dominate the design, or **Broken Frames**, in which the bright tint is used for the squares and triangles so that the brown and green patches take a back seat and, indeed, appear as fragmented shapes across the surface.

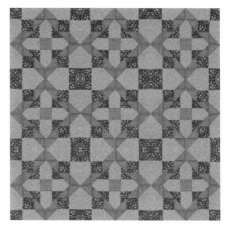

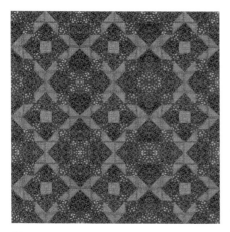

1 **2** **3** **Touch of Scarlet** A really warm, homely color scheme based on shades of deep brown (2) with golden tan (3) forming a background to the scarlet (1), which is a little brighter, so adding a vibrant touch without disrupting the generally comfortable feel of the quilt.

1 **2** **3** **Window Boxes** Geraniums on a windowsill against a gray sky inspired this color scheme, in which the more muted shades of gray (2) and green (3) combine to form a pattern of squares-on-point and crosses, the geranium red (1) patches injecting a cheerful note into what might otherwise be a somber scheme.

1 **2** **3** **Olive Grove** Rich, glowing olive (2) contrasts well with a much darker shade of the same color (1), the pattern being outlined by bright ginger (3) frames in a tasteful, low-key scheme with a very traditional look to it.

Puss in the Corner template This template shows the individual pieces of a block, irrespective of color.

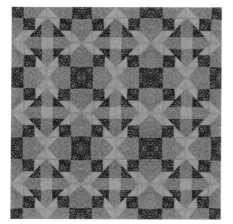 

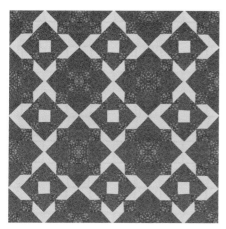 

①②③ Violet Paths There is a subtle harmony in this combination of brown (1), with its hint of purple, and pale violet (3) in the long patches, both set on a background of medium golden brown (2), which highlights the other colors and imparts a slightly opulent atmosphere to the scheme.

①②③ Bright Outlook Dense, warm magenta pink (2) is the heart of this scheme, combining with deep plum (1) to form a harmonious background to the eye-catching pale lavender (3) frames, which stand out as a checkerboard pattern across the quilt.

①②③ Broken Frames Two cool greens, one very pale bluish green (1), the other very dark (3), lend unity to the color scheme, but contrast between the pale green and the rich, dark brown (2) causes the paler, brighter shapes to come forward, giving the pattern a fragmented look.

①②③ In the South A color scheme based on the rich, glowing colors of olive oil (2) and black grapes (1), with darker olive (3) outlining patterns of crosses-on-point in a quilt with a distinctly Mediterranean feel.

shades/**Star of the East**

When shades are used in the piecing of the stars, which are then set on a pale or neutral background, the effect is to generally lighten the mood, **Shaded Harmony** and **Emerald and Amber** being good examples of this. Alternatively, when brighter colors are used in the stars and set on a dark background, the stars acquire added brilliance, as in **Soft Glow** and **Embers**.

1
2
3
Ruby Red Pieced in two slightly somber prints, dark jade green (2) and very dark blue (3), the stars look slightly faceted and seem to sink back into the ruby red (1) in a rich, dense color scheme.

1
2
3
Tangerine Sky The visual illusion of three-dimensional stars, created by using dark and light blue (2, 3) in the rays, is emphasized when they are set against a background of complementary orange (1), making a very striking color scheme based both on shades and the impact of complementary colors.

1
2
3
Soft Glow Tan brown (2) and marmalade orange (3) give the stars their subdued three-dimensional effect, so when placed against a background of deep, midnight blue (1) they glow softly. Blue squares and diamonds make a strong appearance in the design.

Star of the East template This template shows the individual pieces of a block, irrespective of color.

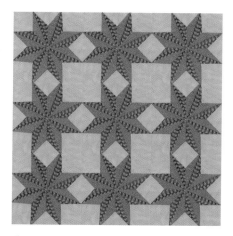

1 2 3 **Shaded Harmony** Aubergine (2) and reddish pink (3) stars contrast strongly with a shell pink (1) background, but because all the colors sit close to each other on the color wheel, the final effect is light and harmonious.

1 2 3 **Embers** Purple (2) and red (3) stars shine brightly against the charcoal (1) background, although the brighter red rays of the stars, glowing like coals, catch the eye first in a dramatic color scheme.

1 2 3 **Emerald and Amber** Amber (2) and emerald green (3) glow together in the stars, but when they are placed on a background of soft, pale grayish green (1) the final effect is elegant and sophisticated.

1 2 3 **Antique Bronze** The three-dimensional effect is clear in these smoky blue (2) and deep purplish blue (3) stars, which are well defined against a background of antique bronze (1), casting a generally opulent, dignified atmosphere over the whole quilt.

shades/**Virginia Star**

In **String of Emeralds**, the Virginia Star makes a real splash as the star points contrast brightly with the dramatic black background, whereas in **Leading Lights** the tones at the edges of the stars contrast less obviously with the dark background, leaving the yellow stars as the main focus. Place shaded stars on a neutral background for a fresh, crisp quilt, such as in **Shaded Lights**.

1 **2** **3** **4** **Shaded Lights** Deep sea green (4) in the centers of the stars blends subtly with the surrounding dark print (3). Diamonds in mid-violet (2), also lifted from the print, give the shaded stars definition against the pinkish cream (1) background, for a fresh and elegant final effect.

1 **2** **3** **4** **Star Attraction** A very cheerful, exuberant scheme is drawn together by the bright yellow (1) background and medium shade of blue (4), the effect being slightly toned down by the addition of brown (3) and grassy green (2) points for the stars.

1 **2** **3** **4** **Misty Stars** A cool gray (1) background imparts a slightly misty aura over the soft shades of plum (2, 3), with the deep sea green (4) at the centers of stars adding a series of slightly brighter focal points.

Virginia Star template
This template shows the individual pieces of a block, irrespective of color.

1 **2** **3** **4** **String of Emeralds** A subtle blend of deep pink (3) and a medium tone pink (4) is given sharp definition by adding emerald green (2) diamond star points. Seen against a black (1) background, the colors have a jewel-like gleam, while the black squares and diamonds are emphasized where the green points meet.

1 **2** **3** **4** **Leading Lights** Bright yellow (4) stars are definitely the leading lights in this scheme, especially when surrounded by complementary kingfisher blue (3). Contrast between the pink (2) star points and purple (1) background is subdued but enough to give the stars definition.

1 **2** **3** **4** **Superstar** Orange (4) stars make a splash when surrounded by deep pine green (3), while acid yellow (2) diamonds show up brilliantly against the dark gray background (1) in a striking and effective marriage of deep shades and bright tones.

1 **2** **3** **4** **Jade Brooches** Khaki (2) and brown (3) blend seamlessly together, isolating the jade (4) stars in the center. When set against a deep purplish blue (1) background a rich, dense scheme emerges, from which the green centers glow.

shades/**Bow Tie**

There is an added dimension to this simply pieced block when inventive use is made of a striped fabric that has been "fussy cut." In **Gray Bias** the resulting textural effect serves to make a harmonious color scheme more decorative and complex. Shades are used in **September Song** to create a slightly melancholy, autumnal mood, relieved by the introduction of russet in a brighter tone, while in **Jade Embellishment** a neutral color is used to brighten the surface and also to emphasize the diagonal elements.

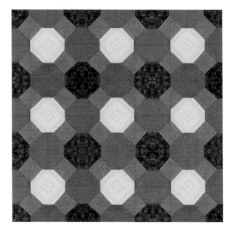

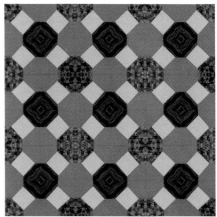

1 2 3 4 Gray Bias Very dark forest green (2) squares resemble a grid with alternating octagons in mottled gray-blue (1) and a matching striped fabric (4) at the intersections. Octagons in a subdued greenish lilac (3) can be read as a background to the other colors.

1 2 3 4 Background Shade Shades of light and medium olive green (2, 3) tend to merge and create a patterned background to indigo blue (1) and yellow (4) octagons. The comparative brightness of the yellow octagons gives them the central role.

Bow Tie template
This template shows the individual pieces of a block, irrespective of color.

1 2 3 4 Golden Glow When bright gold (2) is used for the squares, the grid illusion is emphasized, seemingly set with octagons in a medium tone of emerald green (1) and deep pinkish brown (4). Deep pink (3), toning with the brown, combines with the gold to give a sense of glowing warmth and opulence.

① **Jade Embellishment** Neutral cream (2),
② toning well with spicy ginger (4) and dark tan
③ (3), illuminates and defines the pattern and
④ emphasizes its diagonal bias. The surface is
embellished with octagons in a subdued tone
of jade green (1).

① **September Song** There is a hint of coming
② fall in this combination of nut brown (2), pine
③ green (3), and russet (4), in which the mellow
④ russet octagons provide a series of focal
points and deep indigo (1) adds depth and
discreet contrast.

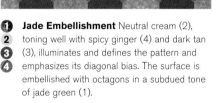

① **Ginger Highlights** A deep, dense
② background is created by the harmonious
③ combination of dark turquoise (2) and navy
④ blue (3). Bright azure (4) and complementary
spicy ginger (1) brighten the surface but
combine with the darker colors to produce a
satisfyingly deep, rich quilt.

① **Sobering Touch** Similar tones of pink (1),
② complementary mint green (2), and yellow (4)
③ give all the shapes pieced in them equal
④ value, so the much darker shade of chocolate
brown (3) provides the main contrast, and at
the same time adds depth and a touch of
sobriety to the scheme.

shades/**Kaleidoscope**

Shaded colors may be subdued, but they can still provide plenty of visual interest if the tones and values used have sufficient brightness and contrast. In **Burnt Cinnamon**, the cinnamon color is slightly more glowing than the other colors, giving a pleasing effect, while in **Forest Fruits** it is the subtly brighter tones of the gray that give contrast. Neutrals can also be used with shades, as seen in **Propeller Blades** and **Surprisingly Modern**. However, notice that the neutrals contain a tint of one of the other colors.

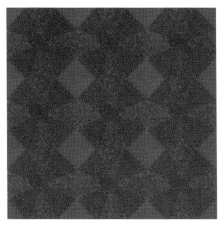

①②③ Surprisingly Modern The combination of neutral oatmeal (1) with reddish brown (3) is typical of homely traditional feeling color schemes, but the introduction of the black (2) print adds depth, and gives the quilt a surprisingly modern look.

Kaleidoscope template
This template shows the individual pieces of a block, irrespective of color.

①②③ Burnt Cinnamon Dark shades of jade (1) and purple (2) become a background for the rich burnt cinnamon (3) diamonds lying over them, which provide the necessary element of contrast to a potentially somber combination. The similar tones of the background colors suggest a shadowy sense of movement.

①②③ Silver Service Medium silver gray (2) juxtaposed to bright sunshine yellow (1) and warm red (3) has a slightly cooling and muted influence, while at the same time seeming to enhance the effects of movement and light in a lively, bracing color scheme.

① ② ③ Traditional Color Scheme Contrast between neutral cream (2) and the other two colors, green (1) and tan (3), both in subtly subdued tones, lightens the surface and at the same time defines the other shapes in a very practical, traditional color scheme.

① ② ③ Propeller Blades Adding a small proportion of neutral creamy oyster (1) highlights the contrast between air-force blue (3) and tan (2), both in subtly subdued tones, lightening the surface and defining the other shapes. Similar tones in the darker colors emphasize the circular movement of the pattern.

① ② ③ Forest Fruits Setting warm, shady mulberry (1) squares into the pattern of cool gray (2) triangles and dark forest green (3) diamonds gives a subtle impression of depth and richness, with the very slightly brighter tone of gray providing just sufficient contrast and definition.

① ② ③ Pale Diamonds Good contrast between the harmonious blues (2, 3) gives maximum effect to the pattern of pale diamonds over dark octagons. A soft, dusky shade of pink (1) gives contrast and a touch warmth, and confirms the generally calm, understated quality of the quilt.

shades/**Lattice and Square**

These quilts use shades in differing proportions to define or subdue elements of the pattern, creating a surprisingly wide range of effects from one design. In **Little Mulberry Squares** the shades are less in evidence than the two other colors and are used to counterbalance the neutral cream. Both **Warm and Cozy** and **Lively Touch** use tones of red to enliven the other, more subdued colors, but because they are in small proportions in relation to the other fabrics, they never dominate.

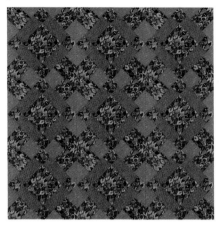

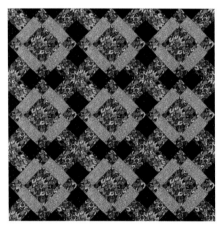

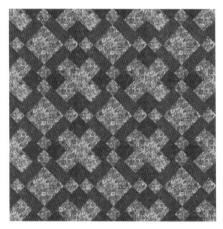

Cool Depths A striking monochrome quilt based on shades of blue. The underlying lattice effect is enhanced by the contrast between medium blue (1) and navy (2), while the use of sky blue (3) in the squares makes them the main focus.

Lattice and Square template This template shows the individual pieces of a block, irrespective of color.

Warm and Cozy Shades of warm pinkish red (2) and donkey brown (3) make a harmonious combination. When olive green (1) is added, in a slightly brighter tone, the underlying lattice effect is emphasized and interest is added, without disturbing the warm and cozy feeling that the quilt imparts.

Orange Grove A deep shade of brown (2) set against orange (1) gives definition to the pattern of crosses and squares, but deep turquoise (3) squares also make their mark against the orange. In this quilt shades are used to tone down the bright orange, but the graphic impact is still strong.

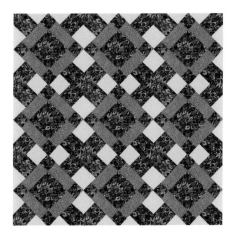

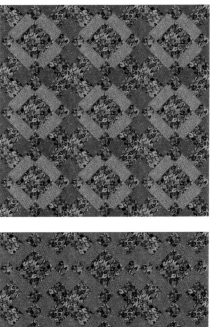

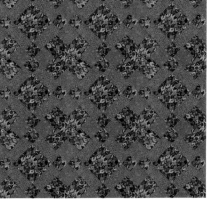

Lifting the Blues Pale yellow (2) set against shades of navy blue (1) and medium blue (3) lightens and brightens the whole surface, while at the same time giving the blues added impact and emphasizing the underlying lattice effect in the design.

Dark Influence Both medium turquoise (1) and olive (3), which has a touch of yellow, gain a little added interest by the juxtaposition of dark slate gray (2), even though only a small proportion of gray is used. The result is a striking but practical color scheme.

Little Mulberry Squares A small proportion of a soft shade of mulberry (2) is used as contrast to the neutral cream (1) and harmonious orange (3) and, being almost complementary to the other colors, makes a pleasing contribution to a light, stylish quilt.

Lively Touch Similar tones for the leafy green (1) and tan (3) give the pattern of alternating squares and crosses discreet definition. Squares in cyclamen pink (2), being a touch brighter in value than the other colors, peep out to add a warm, lively touch.

shades/**Washington Pavement**

Vivid and eye-catching, like **Tangy Yellow** and **Bold Choice**, or diffuse like **Diffuse Harmony** and **Radiating Warmth**, all these quilts rely for their effect on mixing shades with other colors in carefully selected tones and values. Notice that greater contrast between the small squares and the main shapes results in bright, clear definition of those shapes, whereas when contrast is muted, a more peaceful and understated effect is achieved, as in **Blue Streaks** and **Peaceful and Serene**.

❶❷❸ Diffuse Harmony This almost monochrome quilt uses rust (1) and medium gold (3), which both echo colors in the floral print (2), so that all the fabrics tend to merge, with the brightest tone, the medium gold (3), providing necessary contrast and definition; even so, the overall impression is warm and diffuse.

❶❷❸ Tangy Yellow Acid yellow (1) contrasts so strongly with the other two colors, medium tan (2) and pine green (3), that the squares forcefully come forward, although the tan octagons surrounded by lines of green triangles also show up well, in a color combination that is lively and stimulating.

❶❷❸ Blue Streaks A sober and dignified combination of slate gray (1) and mid-tan (2) is considerably enlivened by lines of blue (3) triangles that streak across the surface and make an even greater impression because the blue and tan are more or less complementary.

Washington Pavement template This template shows the individual pieces of a block, irrespective of color.

1 **2** **3** **Bold Choice** Bold and dynamic, this marriage of a deep shade of violet (2) and deep rose (3) looks even more striking when yellow (1), complementary to the violet, is introduced between the octagon shapes.

1 **2** **3** **Peaceful and Serene** Quiet shades of olive (1) and petrol blue (2) form a background to a grid of lighter blue (3) triangles that give a slight lift to the surface but, because they harmonize with the deep blue, don't disturb the generally serene and peaceful mood.

1 **2** **3** **Radiating Warmth** A warm shade of tan (3) is surrounded by a harmonious yellow (1) and tangerine (2) for a scheme in which subdued contrast is used to create muted radiance, so that the quilt is suffused with mellow warmth.

1 **2** **3** **Shady Plum** A really deep, shady plum (2) sets off the bright eggshell blue (3) triangles, while neutral cream (1) squares set between the darker octagons throw them into sharp relief.

shades/**Winding Ways**

Winding Ways always lives up to its name and offers an easy way to create quilts with an element of rhythm and movement. Using color schemes based on shades can also achieve subtle, understated effects while at the same time ensuring that the quilt surface is lively and interesting. In **Subtle Statement**, the colors are harmonious so the necessary contrast is achieved by using a slightly brighter tone of pink. In **Rhythmic Figures**, clear contrast between the two colors results in a strong, clearly defined pattern.

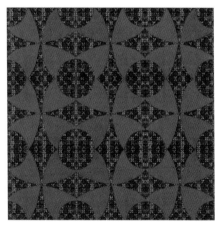

❶ ❷ **Shady Waves** A brownish red (1) background shows subdued contrast with shady blue (2), which contains a hint of gray. The tones of the two fabrics are similar, so the pattern appears elusive and diffuse, but the combination of colors results in a quilt with a subtle richness.

Winding Ways template
This template shows the individual pieces of a block, irrespective of color.

❶ ❷ **Rhythmic Figures** A pleasing combination of shades of petrol blue (1) and olive (2). The olive shapes come forward to catch the eye first because of their subtly brighter value, and good contrast between the two colors emphasizes all the shapes and the rhythmic character of the pattern.

❶ ❷ **Easygoing Quilt** Slightly chalky shades of sage green (1) and plum (2) in similar tones show just enough contrast to reveal the shape and movement of the design, resulting in an easygoing quilt with a pleasingly calm and relaxed mood to it.

1
2 **Sedate and Dignified** A subdued tone of deep-dyed burgundy (2) is set on an olive (1) background, which has just the touch of brightness needed to emphasize all the shapes and movement, resulting in a sedate and dignified color scheme that would look great with a cream décor.

1
2 **Subtle Statement** Dark, misty plum (1) and a subdued tone of deep dusky pink (2) make for a warm and understated quilt in which the subtly brighter tone of pink allows those shapes to come forward.

1
2 **Cross Currents** A mix of medium mint green (1) and a darker shade of blue (2) emphasizes all the shapes and movement inherent in this pattern, in a very cool, refreshing quilt suggesting watery depths and currents.

1
2 **Swirling Leaves** Rich, glowing shades of mid-brown (1) and old gold (2) look harmonious together and give just enough definition to a very subtle and understated quilt with a mellow, autumnal mood.

shades/**Round Table**

You can vary the character of Round Table, with its formal geometric shapes, by playing off the colors in the large segmented circles against those in the small concentric circles. **Antique Gold** and **Refined Harmony** both rely for their effect on a certain harmony between the small circles and one of the background colors. In **Warm Glow** the small circles are the heart of the quilt and determine its character.

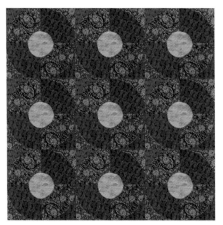

1 2 3 Antique Gold The pleasingly mellow, antique impression created by the main shapes in deep turquoise (1) and a print with a deep rusty red (2) background, is enhanced by the addition of old gold (3) circles, which are the perfect choice for adding sympathetic highlights that underline the antique theme.

Round Table template
This template shows the individual pieces of a block, irrespective of color.

1 2 3 Smart and Stylish A very deep shade of navy blue (1) and complementary mustard yellow (2) look smart and stylish together, and the added circles in deep pinkish brown (3) confirm and enhance a strong, masculine design with a no-nonsense, tailored look to it.

1 2 3 Spruced Up Cream neutral (1) with a very deep shade of plum (2) give crisp, sharp definition and emphasize the checkered effect of the pattern. The gray circles (3) serve to tone down the visual impact just a little by providing restful focal points in a smart, stylish quilt.

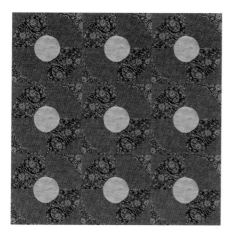

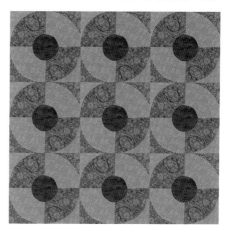

❶ ❷ ❸ Cool Focus Muted contrast between similar tones of mulberry (1) and olive (2) causes the circle shapes to merge and recede a little, although the pattern made by the olive shapes emerges, even if in a very understated way. Grayish mint green (3) circles provide cool focal points.

❶ ❷ ❸ Warm Glow Shades of dusky pink (1) and turquoise (2) form a dense, rich background and, being in similar tones, exaggerate the effect of the contrast with the brighter peach (3) circles that lighten the surface with a warm glow.

❶ ❷ ❸ Refined Harmony Softened shades of coffee (1) and air-force blue (2) look tasteful and sophisticated, and chocolate brown (3) circles, harmonizing with the coffee, confirm and enhance this impression.

❶ ❷ ❸ Pale Moons Contrast between cool misty blue-gray (1) and deep plum (2) has strong impact, but neutral pearl gray (3) circles are closer to the blue in color and tone so the lighter, brighter colors determine the overall character of the quilt.

shades/**Japanese Fan**

Combining shades with tints can be very effective, but colors must be carefully considered. It is a good idea to choose colors that are fairly close on the color wheel, like those in **Shades in Harmony**, where the effect is based on light/dark contrast between various shades and tints in the pink range, with green introduced just for variation. **Unity and Balance** works because two harmonious colors are balanced with two different ones.

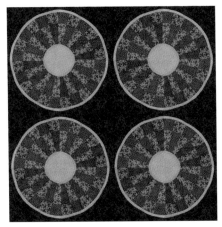

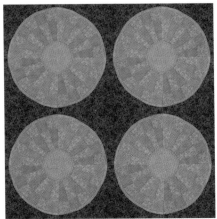

①
②
③
④
Glint of Gold Fans pieced in rust (2) and a floral print on a gold background (3) have a decidedly opulent look, which is enhanced by gold (4) rims and circles. When the fans are set on a deep royal blue (1) background, the overall mood is rich and exotic.

①
②
③
④
Relaxed Mood Soft, chalky shades of sage (2) and pinkish lilac (3) give the fans muted definition. Deepest plum (4) is used to define them against the equally muted dusky rose (1) background, but the gently relaxed overall mood prevails.

Japanese Fan template
This template shows the individual pieces of a block, irrespective of color.

①
②
③
④
Soft Touch Lilac (2) and coral (3) fans are bright and vibrant and gain even more impact when set on a dark brown (1) background. A subdued shade of olive (4) gives a slightly softer touch to the overall effect.

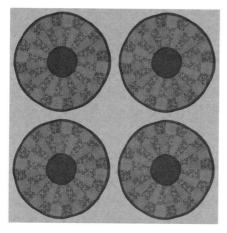

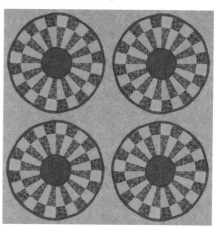

①②③④ Shades and Tints Salmon pink (2) and dove gray (3) make soft, pretty fans that gain a little more weight when set with strongly contrasting indigo (4) circles and rims set against a background in a medium tint of mustard yellow (1).

①②③④ Shades in Harmony Deep-dyed aubergine (1), rose pink (3), and pinkish lilac (4) are harmonious together, while sage green (2) in the fans is used to give color variation without obtruding too much on the coherence and harmony of the scheme.

①②③④ Unity and Balance Light and dark tones of apple green (2, 3) make harmonious fans, so when set with two other harmonious colors, orange (1) and dark tan (4), the quilt has a pleasing sense of unity and balance.

①②③④ Coffee Cream Background Contrast between very dark aubergine (2) and medium turquoise (3) emphasizes the strong, checkered pattern of the fans, and pinkish red (4) rims and center circles give them even more impact against the softer, more subdued tone of the coffee cream (1) background.

shades/**Friendship Fan**

Combine dark, somber colors to create beautiful, rich schemes holding a suggestion of fall and winter. Quilts like **Stylish in Brown** and **Heather Moor** are soft and refined, handsome rather than pretty, while lighter versions, such as **Mulberry Circles** and **Elegant Style** have a quality of quiet elegance. Quilts in this range of colors and tones are eminently suited for use in home décor schemes where they are intended to complement rather than to stand out.

1 **2** **3** **Copper Rings** Copper (3) rings contribute warm focal points to a subdued scheme based on a very pale creamy tone of moss green (1) and a darker mottled print (2). Shapes pieced in the lighter, brighter color come forward strongly to emphasize the angular lines of the design.

1 **2** **3** **Mainly Pink** Dark olive (1) and a subdued shade of complementary fuchsia pink (2) give the fans quiet resonance. Shell pink (3) circles add bright focal points, but by picking up on the darker pink give that color the major role in the quilt.

1 **2** **3** **Stylish in Brown** Both the browns, in tan (1) and a very deep chocolate (2), might look a little dull, but palest green (3) circles are bright enough to lift the surface while at the same time toning well with the other colors, so the final effect is extremely handsome and refined.

Friendship Fan template This template shows the individual pieces of a block, irrespective of color.

1 **Mulberry Circles** Dark forest green (1) and
2 pale peach (2) give crisp, clean definition to
3 the fan blades, while mulberry (3) arcs in a
very deep shade show just enough contrast
with the similarly toned green to give the
circles definition.

1 **Heather Moor** A quiet, subdued shade of
2 misty heather (1) is offset by a smaller
3 proportion of dark peaty brown (2) to evoke
the colors and atmosphere of a Highlands'
landscape, with neutral greenish cream (3)
circles adding a touch of watery light to
the scene.

1 **Elegant Style** An elegant combination of
2 coffee (1) and peach (2) is enhanced by
3 the addition of blue (3) circles in just the
right color and tone to add a little variation
without obtruding on the otherwise
harmonious combination.

1 **Home Décor** This combination of neutral
2 cream (1) and shady olive (2) might seem a
3 little understated, but good contrast between
them ensures strong definition. When tan (3)
circles are added the result is a refined,
tasteful quilt that would look good in a home
décor scheme based on creams and beiges.

APPLIQUÉ BLOCKS

shades/**Bleeding Hearts**

In-built rhythm and movement make it easy to produce stunning quilts with the Bleeding Hearts pattern. Using color schemes based on shades can result in strong, dynamic quilts, like **Spring Promise**, or calmer, more gentle effects such as **Peach Quilt** or **Perfect Harmony**. Emphasizing different elements of the pattern reveals its versatility. Compare **Purple Rings**, where the main impression is of rows of circles, with **Refined Scheme**, where the circles have receded.

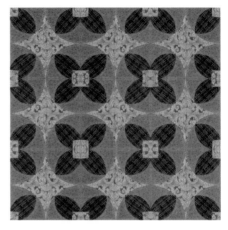

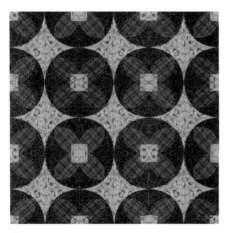

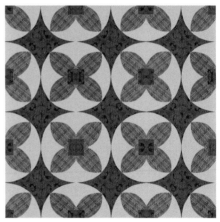

Purple Rings A harmonious scheme based on subdued tones of mauve (1) and reddish purple (3), with a touch of green in a coordinating checked print (2) for variation. Contrast between the pale and dark mauves results in a strong pattern of rings divided by curve-sided squares.

Bleeding Hearts template This template shows the individual pieces of a block, irrespective of color.

Classic Red and Black A classic combination of red (3) and black (2) can't fail to make a dramatic impression. Adding medium gray (1) softens the impact just a little, but this is still a very strong, assertive color scheme in which all the shapes have clear definition.

Spring Promise Palest primrose (3) circles combined with sober earthy shades of chocolate brown (1) and olive (2) hint of early spring. A touch of yellow in the olive ensures a sense of balance and harmony.

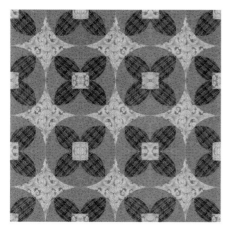

(1) (2) (3) Red Background Strong contrast between curve-sided squares in dusky pink (1), alternating with dark turquoise (2) petal shapes, creates a strong pattern, which stands out well from the soft red (3) background. The subtle contrast between pink and red means that the illusion of circles is played down.

(1) (2) (3) Peach Quilt A soft, graceful quilt in which a muted plum (1) forms curve-sided squares between peach (3) circles set with olive green (2) petal shapes. Olive and plum are in similar tones so the circles in brighter peach are more prominent.

(1) (2) (3) Refined Scheme Deep-dyed brown (2) petal shapes and dusky yellow (1) curve-sided squares seem to be lying over a background of soft, pale tan (3) in a refined scheme in which the harmonious browns are very slightly lifted by the yellow.

(1) (2) (3) Perfect Harmony A harmonious marriage of medium gray-blue (1), pale gray (2), and navy (3) gives perfect definition to all the shapes and emphasizes the rhythmic quality of the design in a beautifully balanced monochrome quilt.

shades/**Dutch Tulips**

With the Dutch Tulips pattern, the colors and tones of the background fabrics have a decisive influence on the final outcome. Manipulate this fact to get the desired look for your quilt. In **Lovely Black Eyes**, the whole effect is dense and rich because it is based strongly on the puce background, with other colors chosen to echo it. **Staying Calm** achieves its peaceful atmosphere from placing subdued tones on a placid bluish gray background, while in **Quiet Good Taste** the background sets the tone.

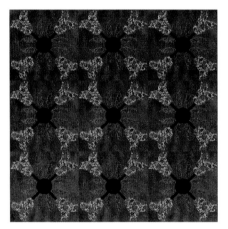

❶
❷
❸
❹
Lovely Black Eyes A significant proportion of red in the paisley print (2) picks up on the glowing puce (1) of the background, so the overall mood is warm and dense, with black (4) emphasizing that impression. Shady blue (3) leaf shapes serve as an unobtrusive backup.

Dutch Tulips template
This template shows the individual pieces of a block, irrespective of color.

❶
❷
❸
❹
Background Light A medium tone of powdery greenish yellow (1) forms lantern shapes that give background light to dusky rose (2) and harmonious purple (4), with mint green (3) giving discreet contrast.

❶
❷
❸
4
Spotlights A gentle shade of gray-blue (1) sets a subdued and calm background to indigo (2) flower heads and pine green (3) leaf shapes. Pale daffodil yellow (4) circles lend splashes of light.

1 **2** **3** **4** **Staying Calm** Florets in grayish tones of sage (3) and blue (4), alternating with soft candy pink (2) flower heads, float across the pale gray-blue (1) surface. There is sufficient contrast to define the shapes, but none of the colors are bright enough to disturb the tranquil mood.

1 **2** **3** **4** **Strong Competition** A strong, well-balanced design in which purplish gray (2) on a background of pale grayish lilac (1) makes a strong visual impact, but yellow (4) centers and stems with turquoise (3) leaves compete for attention.

1 **2** **3** **4** **Quiet Good Taste** A refined, balanced scheme based on combining and contrasting harmonious colors in two different ranges—deep rust (1) and pale coffee (2), and medium and dark olive (3, 4). Although the coffee is bright enough to come forward, all the tones convey an impression of quiet good taste.

1 **2** **3** **4** **Dash of Aqua** Soft orange (1) in a medium tone provides a glowing background for deepest navy (2) and cocoa brown (3). A dash of aqua in the centers contrasts strongly with the orange and gives the quilt a lively, vigorous look.

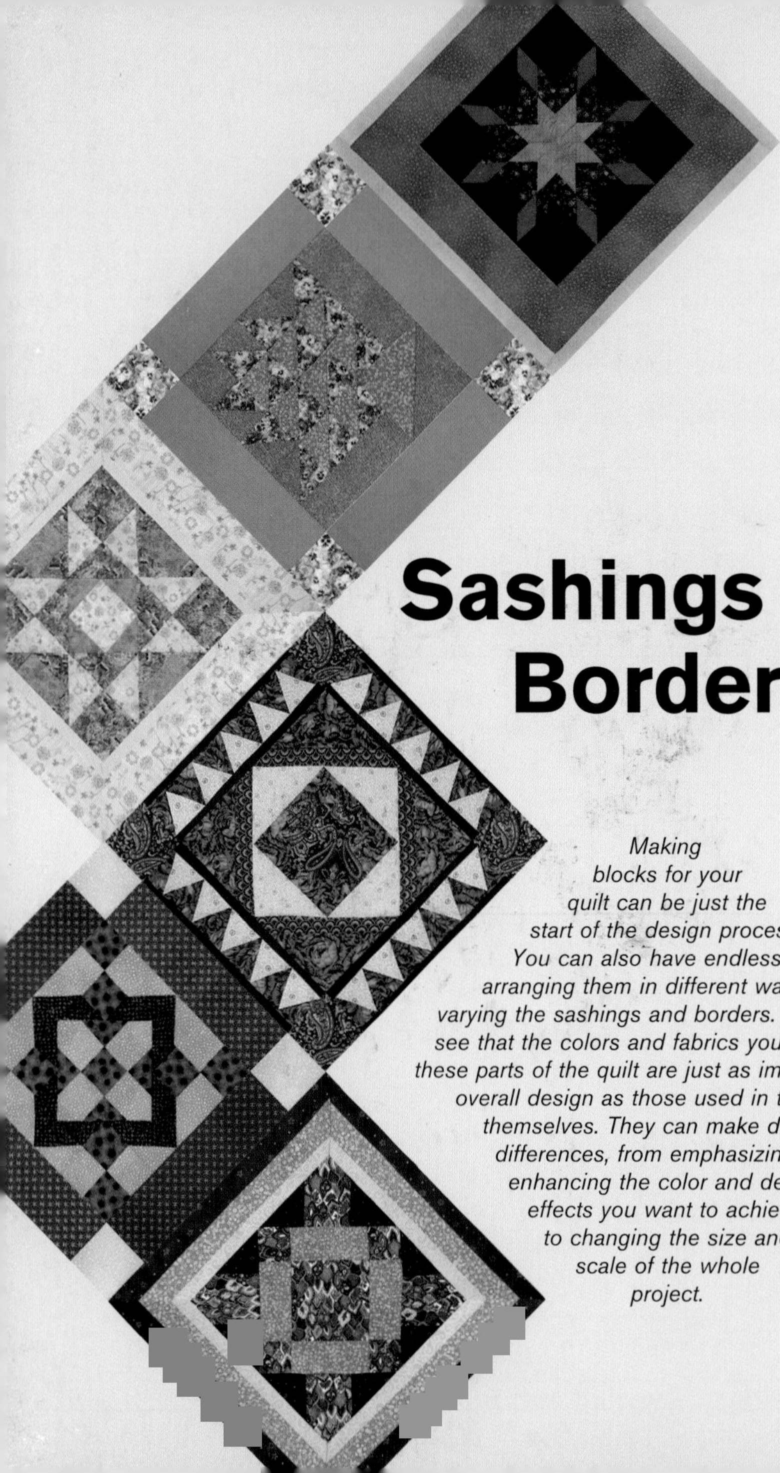

Sashings and Borders

Making
blocks for your
quilt can be just the
start of the design process.
You can also have endless fun
arranging them in different ways and
varying the sashings and borders. You'll soon
see that the colors and fabrics you choose for
these parts of the quilt are just as important to the
overall design as those used in the blocks
themselves. They can make dramatic
differences, from emphasizing and
enhancing the color and design
effects you want to achieve,
to changing the size and
scale of the whole
project.

Blocks don't always need to be set side by side in rows. Try arranging them "on point"— that is, diagonally across the quilt surface— or alternating them with plain, unpieced blocks of another color. For the unpieced blocks, you could choose a fabric which enhances or underlines your basic color idea and then embellish them with a fancy quilting pattern.

Sashings

Blocks are often set with "sashings," which are strips of fabric that separate the blocks, often with square patches where the sashing strips meet, known as "corner posts." Sashings can be used to vary the design of the quilt and they offer another opportunity to change or influence your quilt's color effects—for example, plain calico sashings always look in keeping on a quilt where you want to create a homey, traditional feel.

Sashings
Yellow posts have been used to good effect here. The bold, clean-cut colors and design of the block are complemented by the addition of a plain border in mottled gray/black. The yellow posts pick up on tiny dots of yellow in the green fabric and enhance the generally vibrant effect. A mottled fabric is preferable here to plain black, which would be too stark and might overpower the design.

Borders

Not every quilt needs a border, but if you decide that your design will be enhanced by adding one, you need to be aware of the effects the colors in the border will have on those in the rest of the quilt, because perceptions of color are affected by the colors that surround them. If, for example, your quilt is based mainly on one particular color, it may be enhanced by adding a border which reflects that color. On the other hand, for a quilt that features several colors, you may need to consider which of them you want to emphasize and bring out, since the color of the border will attract other similar colors in the quilt and cause them to stand out.

The tendency for similar colors to attract each other is a particularly important consideration in scrap quilts where many different colors have been used; add a blue border and all the blues will stand out; add

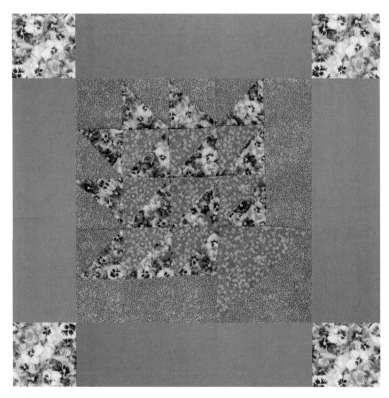

Plain border
When a plain blue border is placed directly against the complementary orange fabric, it has a restful influence on an otherwise rather busy design. Although the blue border brings out the blue in the centers of the blocks, corner posts in the floral fabric break up the border so that it enhances rather than overwhelms the design.

a green border and the greens will pop out. You can use this method to give a sense of unity to even the most eclectic selection of fabrics.

There are several styles of border to choose from, each with its own technique and special effects. In the simplest border, plain strips of fabric are added to top, bottom, and sides of the completed quilt top, either repeating a fabric which is in the main field or adding a different fabric which will complement those in the quilt. When adding a repeat fabric, notice if any patches of it will be directly juxtaposed to the border, in which case they will tend to merge and the impact of the shapes will be lost. In this case, the thing to do is to insert a very narrow strip of another color between the main body of the quilt and the border to separate them.

Double borders, with two different border fabrics, can be very effective when you want

Double border
The red in the block is proportionately less in relation to the other colors, but it gains importance in the design when a red border is added. A narrow border of lime green, echoing the center star, serves to draw the whole scheme together.

to emphasize a particular color combination. They look best when the corners are mitered—that is, finished with a diagonal line at each corner, exactly like a picture frame. Pieced borders can also be an ideal way to add both color and complexity to your quilt.

Finally, don't forget the option of adding appliqué borders to your quilt. This is a very popular and time-honored way of finishing and embellishing a quilt, and many quilt masterpieces, both traditional and contemporary, triumphantly demonstrate this. By adding a border in which colors, shapes, and motifs complement those in the main field of the quilt, you can turn a simple quilt into a work of art!

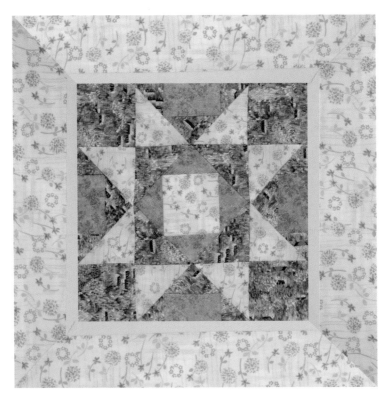

Double border: thick and thin
The narrow yellow border separating the main block from the repeated green fabric of the border adds to the generally light, fresh feel of the quilt.

Mitered, strip-pieced borders
The mitered, strip-pieced borders here feature two of the fabrics used in the center block, while a narrow strip of aqua picks up on hints of that color elsewhere and outlines the main block, introducing a note of lightness and brightness. Using the darker fabric for the outer border effectively frames and draws together the entire scheme.

Pieced border
This basically simple design gets added richness and interest when the triangles of the pieced border, repeating two colors in the main field, pick up and emphasize the strong geometric design of the blocks. This effect is underlined by framing the border in narrow strips of plain black.

Bibliography

ALBERS Joseph *The Interaction of Color* Yale University Press, 1975

ALLEN Jean *Designers' Guide to Color 3* Chronicle Books, 1986

BIRREN Faber *Color: A Survey in Words and Pictures* Citadel Press, 1963

BIRREN Faber *Creative Color* Schiffler, 1987

BIRREN Faber *The Symbolism of Color* Citadel, 1988

BLAKE Wendon *The Color Book* Watson-Guptill, 1981

BYER Jinny *Color Confidence for Quilters* The Quilt Digest Press, 1992

EISEMAN Leatrice *Pantone Guide to Communicating with Color* Grafix Press Ltd, 2000

ITTEN Johannes *The Art of Color* John Wiley, 1997

PENDERS Mary Coyne *Color and Cloth. The Quiltmaker's Ultimate Workbook.* The Quilt
  Digest Press, 1989

McKELVEY Susan Richardson *Color for Quilters* Yours Truly Inc, 1984

STOCKTON James *Designers' Guide to Color* Chronicle Books, 1984

STOCKTON James *Designers' Guide to Color 2* Chronicle Books, 1984

WONG Wucius *Principles of Color Design* Van Nostrand Reinhold, 1997

Internet Resources

There are many lists of recommended books on color on the Internet, including the following:

www.nitaleland.com/books/colorbooks.htm

www.colormatters.com/biblio.html

Suppliers

Thread

Coats & Clark
30 Oatewood Drive, Suite 351
Greenville, SC 29615
Tel: 864-234-0331
www.coatsandclark.com

Guterman of America
PO Box 7387
Charlotte, NC 28241
Tel: 888-488-3762
www.guterman-us.com

Kreinik Mfg Co, Inc
3106 Timanus Lane, Suite101
Baltimore, MD 21244
Tel: 800-537-2166
www.kreinik.com

Sulky of America
3113 Broadpoint Drive
Harbor Heights, FL 33988
Tel: 800-874-4115
www.sulky.com

YLI Corporation
161 West Main Street
Rock Hill, SC 29730
Tel: 800-296-8139
www.ylicorp.com

Sewing Machine Manufacturers

Baby Lock, USA
1760 Gilsinn
St Louis, MO 63026
Tel: 800-422-2952
www.babylock.com

Bernina of America, Inc
3500 Thayer Ct
Aurora, IL 60504
Tel: 630-978-2500
www.berninausa.com

Brother International
100 Somerset Corporate Blvd
Bridgewater, NJ 08807
Tel; 800-422-7684
www.brother.com

Elna USA
1760 Gilsinn Lane
Fenton, MO 63026
Tel: 800-848-3562
www.elnausa.com

Husqvarna Viking Sewing Machines
31000 Viking Parkway
Westlake, OH 44145
Tel: 440-808-6550
www.husqvarnaviking.com

Janome America, Inc
10 Industrial Ave
Mahwah, NJ 07430
Tel: 800-631-0183
www.janome.com

Pfaff of America
31000 Viking Parkway
Westlake, OH 44145
Tel: 800-997-3233
www.pfaff-us-cda.com

Quilting Supplies

Clover Needlecraft, Inc
1007 E Dominguez St #L
Carson, CA 90746
Tel: 310-516-7846

EZ Quilting by Wrights
85 South St
West Warren, MA 01092
Tel: 800-628-9362

Fiskars, Inc
7811 West Stewart Ave
Wausau, WI 54401
www.ezquilts.com

Olfa Products Group
1536 Beech St
Terre Haute, IN 47804
Tel: 800-457-2665
www.olfa.com

Prym-Dritz Corp/Ominigrid
14 Westover Ave
Slamford, CT 06092
www.dritz.com

The Warm Company
854 E Union St
Seattle, WA 98122
Tel: 206-320-9276
www.warmcompany.com

Fabric Manufacturers

David Textiles
5959 Telegraph Rd
City of Commerce, CA 90040
Tel: 213-728-8231

E.E. Schenck Co
PO Box 5200
Portland, OR 97208
Tel: 800-433-0722
www.eeschenck.com

Marcus Brothers
980 Avenue of the Americas
New York, NY 10018
Tel: 212-354-8700
www.marcusbrothers.com

P & B Textiles
1580 Gilbreth Rd
Burlington, CA 94010
Tel: 415-692-0422
www.pbtex.com

Robert Kaufman Fabrics
129 West 132nd Street
Los Angeles, CA 90061
Tel: 800-877-2066

Springs Industries/RHC/For
Quilters Only
420 E White St
Rock Hill, SC 29730

V.I.P. by Cranston
469 Seventh Ave
New York, NY 10018
Tel: 212-946-2202

Mail Order Shopping

Clotilde, Inc
PO Box 7500
Big Sandy, TX 75755
www.clotilde.com

Connecting Threads
PO Box 8940
Vancouver, WA 98668
Tel: 800-574-6454
www.conectingthreads.com

Hancock's of Paducah
3841 Hinkleville Rd
Paducah, KY 42001
Tel: 800-845-8723

Keepsake Quilting
Route 25B
PO Box 1618
Center Harbor, NH 03226
Tel: 800-865-9458

Nancy's Notions
333 Beichl Ave
PO Box 683
Beaver Dam, WI 53916
Tel: 800-833-0690

Credits

Quarto would like to thank the following for allowing images to be reproduced:

Key: t = top, b = bottom

The European Art Quilt Foundation www.europeanartquilt.com p18t, p18b
The Husqvarna Viking International Quilt Contest www.vsmgroup.com p7t, p7b, p16b, p28t
The Quilter's Guild www.thequiltersguild.co.uk p17t, p19t
Barbara Howell p27t
Jen Jones www.jen-jones.com p29t

All other photographs and illustrations are the copyright of Quarto Publishing plc. While every effort has been made to credit contributors, Quarto would like to apologize should there have been any omissions or errors—and would be pleased to make the appropriate correction for future editions of the book.